IT'S GOOD TO KNOW
by Randy Bullock
with Dave Balsiger

mm mott media
BOX 236, MILFORD, MI. 48042

All Scriptures are from the King James Version of the Bible.

Some of the names in this book have been changed to protect the individuals involved. The events are absolutely as described.

© *1975 by Randy Bullock and Dave Balsiger*

All Rights Reserved

Printed in the United States of America
Library of Congress Catalog Card Number: 74-27321
International Standard Book Number:
    Hard Cover: 0-915134-00-4   Soft Cover: 0-915134-01-2

DEDICATED TO
Verne and Karen
for loving me
and to
all those readers
who find this book
the path to an eternal Peace.

Acknowledgements

Neither this book nor the change in my life would have occurred without the prayer, fellowship, teaching, friendship, advice, or assistance of the following people:

my brother Verne and his wife Karen
my Mother and Father
Dave and Janie Balsiger
Les and Sally Jones
Peter and Judy Frankovich
Don and Tap Williams
David L.C. Anderson
Bill Brown
Ken Bliss
Chuck Wenger
J. Michael Hooser
Kenette Riggs
Steve Gottry
Robbie Tregenza
Jim Collier
Cliff Barrows
Tedd Smith
Billy Graham
Doug Stiverson
Ed Kane
Barbara Kootz
Pat Prince
Ake Lundberg
Dave Anderson
World Wide Pictures

Cover Photo — From *Isn't It Good To Know,* Courtesy of World Wide Pictures. Back Cover Photo — By Ake Lundberg, Courtesy of the Billy Graham Evangelistic Association.

Introduction

When Randy Bullock dropped out of Wichita's skies into my life, little did I know of the hell this sensitive, frail young man had just come from. Now, as then, he has pulled no punches in writing a hard, real account of his personal odyssey through the 60's and early 70's, in the genre of Datson Radu's *I Ain't Marchin' Anymore*. Randy, however, tells a love story of joy and sorrow which can only be resolved in Christ.

Here is struggle and search for a father's love, for meaning in the context of sex, drugs and revolution. Here is crime and hustling on the streets of New York. Here is the "May Day" march on Washington to overthrow the government. Here is rivalry with a talented brother for the love of Karen. Here is divine intervention and a story of emerging Christian community.

Randy offers a slice of life, his life; unique in his personality and combination of experiences, yet characteristic not only of a generation, but of the longings of every human heart.

Randy is one of the finest acting talents in Hollywood, and one of the most sensitive spirits I know. Be prepared to be jolted, entranced, and lifted as he tells his story.

Don Williams
Lecturer in Religion
Claremont Men's College
Author of *Call to the Streets*

1

I SAT NEXT to the window, forehead against the pane, looking out through the driving rain and waiting for the DC-10 to lift off from Denver's Stapleton International Airport.

The stewardesses, other passengers, didn't exist. I was blocking off everything except the stirring springtime notes of Beethoven's Sixth Symphony coming through the headset airlines provide.

Everybody aboard this jet was going somewhere, everyone wanted to begin a brand new day. I did, too, but thoughts kept tumbling through my head. Of her. And him.

The plane sat like a rock. Get this plane off the ground! Get it out of Colorado. Hell, I don't care what happens. I don't care if it crashes. Just get it out of Colorado!

I turned up the volume, and the lilting Pastoral Symphony traveled more loudly in my tripping brain. Beethoven loved nature, too.

The Pastoral was Beethoven's *weird* symphony, a trip in itself — dreamy visions of wind, rain, primitive landscapes...

And love. Enduring, eternal love. Pure, tender love.

I remembered the time Karen and I had been watching

birds twittering among the leaves of a sprawling cherry tree in the courtyard below her apartment, in Los Angeles, and I'd thought, "We are the sun and the moon and all things in time."

She had pulled me up from darkness and despair and restored my soul. Up from the valley of evil.

Effervescent, kind, loving Karen. She had made me feel like a man. She brought out the best of my humor, my thoughts. We were always laughing. When I'd go to Karen's apartment, we'd sit and talk and play records and think good thoughts until two in the morning. I never wanted to leave her side, I was so completely happy with her.

She loved music, too.

I had asked her to marry me. She had said yes.

Sitting on the couch in Karen's apartment and looking out at the tree full of singing birds, quiet in each other's arms, totally content with each other, totally lost, totally calm — one.

I sometimes thought, I love Karen more than I love God! Oh, we were audacious! It was perfect.

Then — without the slightest warning, in the very midst of the world's most perfect love and out of a oneness which seemed higher than the Trinity itself, she had broken the news to me. "Verne and I are going to get married this coming Sunday."

My brother Verne — and Karen, the two people I cared most about in the world. How could it be?

Karen, Karen . . . She was everything I loved. Life, sunshine, springtime, flowers, birds, even motorcycles!

The pain of the Pastoral throbbed through the headset. Oh, get this plane off the ground! Tear off this heavy bird weighted down on the rocky ground and lift it up, up, up.

The engines revved finally, as the fourth movement came alive in my head, and the plane began to taxi. Then, on a roaring swell of music, it blasted off the planet and circled west, climbing, climbing. . .

IT'S GOOD TO KNOW

The fifth movement came on, and I gazed down at the foothills, on a pastoral mountain scene and a road, winding, upward.

I seemed to recognize it, and as the music soared with beauty and color, I followed the road till it ended at the little country church.

I could barely see the cars parked around, the cars of the wedding guests, and I knew, without looking at my watch, that it was noon. They were getting married now, this very minute. My brother, Verne, and Karen.

Karen . . . Oh God, Karen! I turned my head away from the window and cried.

Then my mind exploded. I hit my fist into my palm. "I hate you! I hate Verne! *I hate God!*"

There couldn't be a God. He wasn't real. No god would allow this to happen. I'd take the devil, because the pain I felt now was worse than my deepest despair, my most freaked-out trip, the worst that had happened to me in New York, the worst motorcycle crash. All of it was nothing compared to this. No thanks, God. I'll take Hell.

The only thing to do now was try to forget, try to think about the future, about my career, my new career. A new beginning.

My new beginning was in California.

I was going to begin a new role. A role in a feature motion picture.

I had the part of a preacher in the World Wide Pictures' production of *Time to Run.*

Ironic! I was supposed to preach to a bunch of hippies, about love. About Jesus and love!

I would try to do my best. This was my first big break in films. But it would have to be a good acting job. Because I no longer believed in Jesus and love.

I pulled down the shade to shut out Colorado and Karen, turned off the headset. I wanted sleep bad, but the past came up at me, my life began to flash before my closed eyes.

2

I WAS STANDING on top of a 14,000-foot mountain in the Rockies, an hour or so west of the Denver suburb where we lived. I must have been about nine or ten, and looking at the glory before my saucer eyes, I felt as though I was looking down at the entire world. At this altitude, after the long, long climb upward with my father, I had gulped the cold air in the biggest lungfulls I could get.

Along flat stretches of rocks and ledges beneath us, in cup-like declivities and valleys, and in mountain shadows, snow still clung to the rocks. On rock not veiled by snow, reindeer moss softened the stone facades, glistening with frost under the bright sun which promised warmth, but even in summer left this upper world so frigid not even pines could rise.

The world below the rocks and ledges seemed to stretch out forever westward, moving in mists. And there was an eagle! The first I had ever seen. I felt lightheaded as though I floated, suspended, over the vast scene, even as the eagle took flight and, for a moment, hung absolutely motionless in the stark blue. I knew what that eagle felt like. Totally free.

But, then, too, I was proud to be hanging onto my father's big hand. I was glad to have a father who would climb a mountain with me. And here we were, the two of us, on top

IT'S GOOD TO KNOW

of the world. Of all the things we did when I was young, it was a time that would never be forgotten — or equaled.

"Randy! Randy! Randy!" Everyone was shouting. "How does it feel to be a teenager? Hey, Rand, have you started to shave yet?" Doug Stiverson yelled over the din of the record player. Doug was my best friend, but tonight he was a needler, like the rest of the kids I had invited to a record hop to help me celebrate.

Moving to a larger house in a neatly laid-out tract, was supposed to have been a move up for our family. Our new three-bedroom pad in Littleton was only five minutes by bike from the scenes of my early childhood, yet just that shift in geography had made me uneasy.

The record was repeating, "Go away, Little girl," but as I guided Brenda over to the punch bowl, I said, "That doesn't mean you, baby. Come on and have a taste of the punch before everyone discovers it."

She took one sip and shrieked, "Randy! How did you get away with that?"

Brad had happened to stop the record just before Brenda yelled, making the room suddenly quiet. They all heard and rushed the punchbowl.

"Hey, Rand, this is the grooviest record hop we've had this year!" one of the girls exclaimed. It made me feel good to know I was one of the 'in' gang. I had done all the right things my first year at Euclid Junior High.

After the party, I thanked Dad and Mom and went to my room and just lay on the bed listening to my thoughts. I was thirteen! And now I seemed to have a label. The realization shimmered in my vodka-titillated brain: *I* was a teenager! While waiting for sleep, I decided this night was the beginning of the rest of my life.

From now on, I wouldn't be able to be alone and be myself. I had an image to maintain. The group had me.

I decided to let my hair grow really long, to wear freaky clothes, to hang loose. If I was to be accused of freaking out with the Beatles, expected to buy Beatle wigs, shoes, clothes, the whole bit, then I decided that Randy Bullock would do it in a big way.

During the next few weeks, I concluded that school was also one of those two-way experiences. I had been put into some honor classes and for a while had dreams of setting myself up for the Air Force Academy, until I discovered how much it cost in studying and pleasing parents and teachers. I was a great note-taker in class, but seldom studied. One of the things that discouraged me was the way history was presented — they could probably make it more dull, but it was hard to see how. *Current* history was what I dug, and I was a great admirer of John Kennedy. To me, he represented class and change and a vigorous approach to all our problems.

Escapades with my friends were more enticing than burying my nose in books, and I was motivated toward shop, where I could be active. Brad, Barry, Doug, and a couple of other guys, and girls, were my teachers, and we learned much more that year than our parents ever imagined.

How could our parents know what we were doing, anyway? My parents were always gone, doing the work of the church. My mother had been raised a Mormon, and my father, who had joined the Mormon Church only a few years before, was making up for lost time. Like my sister Gloria, 22, and my two brothers Wayne, 19, and Verne, 16, church had never meant that much to me.

But to my parents, it was everything.

Every night of the week it was something: bookwork, ceremonies for my dad, ladies' guild for mom. Sometimes they would leave us alone to go on trips. For a long time I wished they would take half as much interest in me as they

IT'S GOOD TO KNOW

did in their church, but eventually I began to see that there were certain advantages: I didn't have to sneak around; I could drink and smoke right in the house.

My new friends and I didn't agree with the idea of church at all. We thought it a lot of foolishness, that people went about their religion the wrong way. I didn't like the games they played, the holier-than-thou charades.

The Fourth of July was a good way to kick off summer, but carefree summer days in Littleton were not so carefree unless you had some money. I got a job caddying for the Cherry Hills Country Club.

Barry and I made extra money on the links by taking the "duck" caddies, the juniors, for all they were worth in the caddy yard, playing poker and hearts. Barry and I ran the show, dealing the cards and lording it over the younger ones. We maintained our image by smoking cigars — Tiparillos.

Off and on during the whole summer, Barry and I labored and lazed in the grass as golfers chased their balls from hole to hole. It was a perfect kind of job, outdoors in the sunshine.

I liked the way the country club set lived, and it reinforced my passion to be in the "in" crowd. I was succumbing to the philosophy that the best things in life cost money and that it was very, very important to have all the things the best people had. It would even be permissable to steal. Also, I was beginning to doubt the propaganda that America was always right. Certainly it was wrong on the question of civil rights, as Martin Luther King was demonstrating. I can remember my father saying "Boy, those colored boys sure play good ball, don't they?"

I wanted to say, "*What* color, Dad? Call them black, green, or purple, but don't call them colored!"

Mom and Dad were busier than ever in the church, and there was even less time for us to be together. My father had given up asking me to attend the before-school seminars that started at six in the morning. "Do it for us," Dad and Mom coaxed, but finally I just flatly refused, calling this kind of appeal emotional blackmail.

I thought the church people were two-faced. Whenever I did manage to make a Sunday, they would be friendly and cheerful, shaking hands, putting on a real show. Later they would say to my mom, "When's your kid going to quit playing his long-haired game?"

That my parents would put up meekly with this kind of comment, follow these people around, and get more and more involved with them bothered me. They didn't even let me in on what was going on. I had only the haziest notion of what they were doing or why they were doing it until one Saturday night, on my way to bed, I paused to rap on my parents' door to say my usual good night.

"Just a minute, son," Dad called out. "There's something your mother and I want to tell you. Rand, I'm going to be made a Bishop in the church tomorrow morning. I'd like you to come. Will you?"

I gulped. Just like that! I shifted from one foot to the other, my hand on the doorknob. What could I say? Just like that, my dad tells me he is going to be some bigwig in the church. It must have been something he had been preparing for, for a long time. Why hadn't he mentioned it somewhere along the way? Why hadn't he told his kids about his dreams?

Mom finally broke the silence. "You haven't answered," she said. "I hope that now your dad is going to be a Bishop, we can depend on you to at least show him the respect of coming to see him installed."

Social blackmail again. You can't look bad for your parents.

I did respect my father. But I didn't know how to tell him. I was hurt that he hadn't thought enough of me to tell me in advance, not just spring it like this at the last minute, and

IT'S GOOD TO KNOW

then be disappointed if I didn't want to come, or couldn't.

I thought then and there that I wasn't going to allow his position in the Mormon Church to force me into going to church. If it hasn't got it for me, don't ask me to try to accept it.

But in the end, I went because I loved my dad, even if there was no longer any way to tell him. And after that, my parents were home even less.

In November came the biggest shock, the most dramatic and damaging shock of my young life. Doug and I were whispering to each other in American history class one morning, figuring out how we were going to get by with not having done our homework. Just then the door swung open and one of the teachers came in, his face white as he handed a note to our teacher, Mr. Lane.

Mr. Lane peered at the note, then stepped back, as though something had hit him. The class became dead still. In a hoarse voice he muttered, "The President's been shot."

That night, stunned from the news reports, it seemed to me that I had been struggling against the belief that we were living in an era of rampant oppression and injustice, even though I myself was trending toward that kind of lawlessness of mind and deed which had been building up to JFK's assassination. Until now, there had been hope. I might have pulled out. President Kennedy might have found the way out and upward, for the nation, for people like me.

But when John Kennedy died, a shadow descended over the land. . .

3

ON A MAY MORNING in 1964, thirteen people assembled from different directions, all carrying what looked like white robes. One stood out from the rest. He was carrying a large unpainted cross.

"Bring that can of gas over here," he said curtly. A figure hurried to obey. The leader laid the cross down on the ground and poured gasoline over it, then turned to the others. "Get your robes on. Cover your faces. Keep your hoods on." He paused. "We can't risk being recognized."

Then the cross was ablaze. The figures jumped back. The leader held the flaming, smoking cross up and away from his body with a piece of asbestos wrapped around the base to protect his hands. With the burning cross at the front of their column, the white-hooded figures filed two abreast down the steep hill. As they approached the business district, they reformed into a single file down the center of the street and continued their slow, deliberate march. Men on their way to work gaped, cars pulled close to the curb, their drivers craning their necks, women on the sidewalk stopped and gasped.

The marchers passed through the business district and then straight onto the Euclid Junior High School campus. Then, the smoking cross was hurled down on the grass and

IT'S GOOD TO KNOW

the individuals in the column rushed off into school buildings, flinging off robes as they ducked into corridors. In a matter of seconds, the Army of Thirteen had vanished into thin air.

A few of them had been recognized by students or faculty members before they could hide their robes.

The Principal had arrived just in time to see the end of the procession. By the time he got to his office, his phones were ringing off the hook. He was trying to explain to the mayor that Euclid was not harboring a junior auxiliary of the Klu Klux Klan, when his secretary came rushing in. "Did you see them? Do you know who that was in the lead?" she shouted. "That was Randy Bullock with the cross." She shook her head. "He put on a real show this time!"

By the time the Principal reached us, several teachers and some of the short hairs had cornered all but two or three of the ghostly group. I was leaning against a bank of lockers with a bunch of yelling kids circling me, staring at the tail of the robe sticking out from the bottom edge of my locker.

We were all marched into the Principal's office and told to stay there. "What're they so uptight about, anyway?" Doug said, trying to keep the snicker out of his voice. "I thought that was quite a performance, myself."

I shrugged. "I didn't think they'd get so upset. I thought they'd think it was funny."

The whole thing was a revelation to me of how seriously people took themselves. So accustomed were they to the absolute sacredness of their routine patterns, that they flew apart when anything unusual happened. I was astonished at the extent to which fear and hatred and guilt stabbed men's hearts at the slightest reminder of their injustice. This was my first, unintentional, participation in a demonstration, and I was awed by it.

Finally, the Principal came in and shut the door behind him. "Now!" he exploded. "Would you mind telling me what on earth got into you kids to dress up in sheets, light a cross, and march through town and onto the campus?" He glared at me, his face red.

"Well, ah, it's Choice Day," I replied meekly, reminding him that this was the occasion during the school year when the students were allowed to come "in costume."

"Choice D. . .?" He swallowed and started over again. "Choice Day! Well, all right, it was Choice Day. Why couldn't you have come as Huck Finns, or George Washingtons or something?" He spluttered to a stop, then slammed his fist down on the desk as the phone rang again. "This'll be the hundredth call I've gotten this morning! Oh, we'll be famous, boys. You know, someone got your picture coming down Euclid Street. I can just see the paper . . ."

He went on and on. After dire threats of expulsion, restrictions, even prosecution, we were all finally told to go home and stay there until notified.

I had already been in the Principal's office for several minor offenses, but had always managed to get back in his good graces. Would I ever be able to live this caper down? I trudged on home still amazed at the fuss. All I had intended was a simple joke, a little fun to break the monotony.

After a few days at home and another talk with the Principal, the world returned more or less to normal. For the rest of that semester, I tried to be helpful and useful to the faculty and administration and gradually the whole affair was forgotten.

Meanwhile, I found the incident had put me in the limelight and won me admiration among my more weird friends and fellow students. My girlfriend, Barbie, was very impressed. She liked adventure, and anything exciting was her "thing."

Barbie had been my girlfriend ever since the eighth grade, though I had to share her with Barry. She was four feet, eleven inches tall and had long black hair. A lively, sparkling and very excitable girl.

Barry and I had met her at the movies. We used to go

IT'S GOOD TO KNOW

there Friday nights to meet girls from other schools, and one night Barbie had sat next to me. We'd hit it off right from the start. Her initials were "B.A.D.," and she went right along with whatever Barry and I wanted to do.

By the time graduation from ninth grade was upon us, I knew I'd be glad to go into high school. I was surprised when I was asked to set up a committee for the ceremony itself. My intensive public relations work to get back into the good graces of the Principal had paid off. He gave me free rein to organize it, which included choosing a place, putting on a show, setting up the protocol for the continuation ceremony, scheduling and checking the speeches, lights, everything. Drama was what I dug most in the world, and we had ourselves a first-class graduation, outside, under the stars.

Three hundred ninth graders came down the aisle between folding chairs. We wound our way to the front row of seats. As a number of us took our places on the platform along with the speakers, I couldn't help being impressed and proud of the work that had gone into the program. The better side of my nature responded to everything with an emotional tug, as I said goodbye to Euclid Junior High on the night of graduation.

A few days after school was out, I noticed an announcement in the paper, inviting people to tryouts for the musical, *The Unsinkable Molly Brown*. The play was part of the school district's summer interscholastic drama festival directed by Littleton High's Gil Oden, a teacher who already knew me from some of my junior high activities. My brother, Verne, had had a part in a musical, and I was thrilled seeing him in a singing part in *Brigadoon*.

"That's what I want!" I exclaimed. Any chance to try out would do, even if I ended up working the lights. It really got to me when, after appearing at the high school for the tryouts, I was selected for a singing part as one of the brawling miners in the chorus. The show was going to be staged in August. We'd have all summer to rehearse, going at least twice a week.

Everything was going beautifully, and I was burning with anticipation when suddenly, on July 16, the heavens opened up. A cloudburst over the mountains sent a twenty-five foot crest of water roaring down through town. A small dam broke. A flash flood thundered into the space between the two main rivers, the Platt and the Snake, then converged on Palmer Lake.

Having just stocked his warehouse, Dad had a huge inventory of refrigeration equipment and supplies on hand. When the Platt River overflowed, water and mud seeped into the warehouse. There was muck and ooze everywhere. Dad stood there hip-deep in it all and looked sad-eyed at his ruined business.

"Do you have flood insurance, Dad?"

"Flood insurance? In Denver? Who has flood insurance in Denver? It never floods in Denver." Dad's mouth was grim.

The day after the flood, several of Dad's friends came over to help him clean up the mess. I pitched in, using a water hose to try to clear the mud out of the air conditioning units. People everywhere were swabbing out and moving things to higher ground.

The next few weeks I stayed by Dad's side everyday, trying to help him pick up the pieces, while *The Unsinkable Molly Brown* rehearsed without me. For three weeks we worked around the warehouse at what seemed a futile salvaging effort. Then news came that Dad and Mom would be eligible for a government disaster loan. They would be able to start all over again.

Other things worried us besides the flood. Verne had been expelled from Littleton High School during his last year, and Dad had had to send him to stay with one of his friends in Scottsdale, Arizona, where Verne could finish up in a new school.

It was one of those exasperating Establishment type

things, a real fluky. Verne had been in the Madrigal Choir, and a girl was supposed to leave a message for him to wear formal attire for a concert. She didn't. He arrived in his usual levis. The director asked him where the hell his formal attire was. Verne replied, "Oh, bite me!" It was enough to expel him, and no amount of persuasion from Dad would budge the decision.

My other brother, Wayne, was marking time, waiting to go to Vietnam, and we were worried about him getting killed over there. My mother was shaken up, too, about Gloria. She and her husband, Hugh, who had always seemed like such a nice guy to us younger kids, teaching Verne and me to play the guitar, were getting a divorce.

Was God punishing us all? Had he decided, as in Genesis, to remind us of His wrath and power? We'd had no warning about these events, including the flood. Noah at least had been told ahead of time.

4

AFTER A SUMMER away from rules and schedules, I didn't look forward to returning to school. It seemed as though I hadn't had enough time to be alone, to do whatever my impulse dictated. I was restless. The fact that I was going into high school didn't affect me; it would be basically the same old act on a more advanced level.

But I could go out for football. It would give me lots of outdoor time and even excuse me from some classes. I could look forward to a few extra hours away from school and some trips, plus I would get a chance to work with other fellows on a team basis.

I built up great expectations. On the day we were to turn out and hear plans for the year, I dawdled in the locker room, thinking of all the thrills in store for me. I'd show them what I was made of. I could imagine the coach in the huddle, his arms around our shoulders, getting right down to our level, inspiring us.

I had on my expensive new football shoes, one of Dad's gifts in appreciation for helping him in the summer. I felt ten feet tall, ready to hold that football up against my bulging chest, tear down the field, and fly over the crossbar. This would be a great year!

"We're going to do some warm-ups," the coach said.

"Three laps around the field and no shortcuts. Then we'll have a little talk about what's what."

Warm up? Just coming outside was warming up! It was 90 degrees and not a breeze blowing. By the time I'd done the three laps, I was ready to collapse. Coach Ultman had us sit in the burning sun in a wide circle around him.

"Men, on this playing field you work for me," he shouted, turning slowly. When his eye fell on me, holding my football helmet in one hand, pushing my soggy long hair out of my face with the other, he hesitated. He frowned a moment. "The most important thing is this: when you're playing football for me, and you open your mouth and utter a sound that isn't a grunt or a moan or a yell, then all I want to hear is only three things: 'Yes, *sir,* no, *sir,* or I need help, sir.' "

My mouth dropped open. I could still hear my heart pounding in my ears from the running. Sweat was streaming down my neck. I thought, "This is really something! Really a nice greeting for the beginning of the season."

Coach Ultman looked around the circle. "Is that clear?" he said.

"No, sir," I said, standing up. "There is a fourth thing: I quit, sir." I turned on my heel and walked off to the lockers. I didn't stop or turn around. I felt the awed stares of everyone on that field burning into my back.

In the locker room, I got out of my gear and turned it in. When I had changed, I held my nice new football shoes in my hands for a moment. Then I put them down on a bench. Maybe someone else would like to have them.

The one outlet that made me feel most free during this period was riding motorcycles. When we weren't in school, Doug Stiverson and I lived on bikes. I had to rent mine, but Doug had his own, a Yamaha 80.

Motorcycles always fascinated me. They seemed right and natural for me, part of my personality. And they gave me a feeling of confidence, handling all that raw speed and power. Riding them in the dirt, smashing and crashing around trees, taking long "ski" jumps off the tops of hillocks in grassy fields was pure joy. Sometimes Doug and I went far into the wilderness, camping out two or three nights in a row, roaring up and down the trails.

Each day was an adventure. The hills and bike trails and city streets were our playgrounds. We put low gears on Doug's Yamaha 80 and perfected a system for doing spectacular, two-rider wheelies — both of us on the one bike. The driver revved up, then we both threw our balance to the back just at the right moment to lift the front wheel high in the air.

During my first two years in high school, not only was I learning how to handle horsepower, but I was making great strides, from my point of view, in learning a lot about womanpower. I had my own approach to boy-girl relationships and didn't dig the big social functions. My idea was that a good time out with a girl was a personal, private, intimate affair. As far as dates were concerned, I avoided an audience.

I relished being the suave, well-dressed escort, picking girls up at their homes with a bouquet of flowers in my hand, complimenting them, treating them with lavish courtesy and really showing them a quietly enjoyable, adult-type good time. I'd often take them to a nice place for dinner, then to a concert or show, and stop afterward for dessert.

The girl who rewarded me most for the way I treated my dates by making me feel successful and worthy was Valerie. Valerie was blond, pretty, slightly overweight, delicate and sexy. She was straightforward, honest and handled her respectability in such a way that I felt proud when she showed approval of me. I thought of her as perfect "wife material," because, although she was an excellent student, she had an unshakable ambition to be a good wife and mother first and foremost. We confined our romance to kissing and were like Romeo and Juliet.

Yet . . . another part of my nature kept pulling me away;

another kind of girl kept attracting me. Memories of Barbie would stir fires in me that I kept well shielded from Valerie.

One of these nymphs with the grape-stained feet was Kathy, a girl of bold excitement and tantalizing uncertainty, sometimes flowing lazily like a river going nowhere, sometimes suddenly swelling in angry or passionate tides. Kathy brought out the wildness in me, a hot, tropical blood-rain.

I had no resources to fight the temptations into which such felines lured me . . . or into whose depths I so eagerly plunged. My father's church I'd brushed off. There was still no spiritual influence I could accept . . . my mind refused the idea of any Godpower that had a right to insist on moral rules. And I fully accepted sexual pleasure as a legitimate pastime.

A small whisper would sometimes warn me of danger ahead, but I seemed incapable of restraining myself from flying off on the wild side. I was a savage moving to the hammer of rock music which constantly bombarded my mind. I dug the provoking decibels. They inflamed me, seemed to feed a soul hungry for repeated justification for fighting all the imagined oppressions, repressions, frustrations which these same cacaphonies confirmed as they drummed into my head patterns for seemingly impulsive acts of violence in a madness that hovered but a little way ahead.

Observing people around me, adults and the "powers that be," I was rankled by their practice of the double standard, their persistance in attaching importance to appearances. My parents, especially my dad, constantly nagged me to get a haircut, and the high school Principal was at it almost every other week.

Struggling to suppress my resentment, the only thing that held me together — for awhile — was the necessity to work.

Taking girls out and keeping up a wardrobe of two or three good suits and accessories ran into a bundle. I had to keep busy supplementing my allowance. Doug and I got jobs in a restaurant. Doug's grandmother picked us up evenings at five to take us to work and then took us home at one or two in the morning. The hours were too long, and the work took too much out of us to leave any energy for school work. Before long Doug and I switched to jobs at an ice cream store.

Work started me thinking about the future. I seriously began to consider drama as a career. Ever since I could remember, the idea of drama had intrigued me. I made opportunities to put on a show — childhood Fourth of July performances, the KKK fiasco. And drama had something else going for it, less hassle. Theater people treated you as an individual and accepted you whatever way you were.

Though they enjoyed seeing me on stage, my parents were skeptical about drama as a career. "It's going to be a damned poor life if you fail," was Dad's comment. "You can work in community theaters all your life and enjoy it. But you still have to make a living." Mom was afraid my interest in the theater would interfere with college plans.

But at sixteen I was confident an actor's life would be right for me. I didn't have vaulting ambitions. I thought I could make a comfortable living as a character actor, and I was even willing to wait until I was 25 or 30 years old before coming on strong.

Through my first major high school play, during the spring of my sophomore year, I got some unique experience in racial problems. The play, *Early Dawn,* was a heavy Civil War drama written by Dr. Russell Porter, of Denver University. At that time, there was only one black student attending Littleton High, a guy named LeRoy. He played the role of a slave. It was only a two-minute speaking part, but important and a tear-jerker.

I tried out for the play, but being only a sophomore, I had to settle for a few small lines in the chorus.

IT'S GOOD TO KNOW

Not having much of my own material to rehearse, I'd practice some of the black dialect just for fun while waiting for my cues.

About a week before the show was to open, LeRoy, who was having family problems, suddenly dropped out. Mr. Oden, the high school drama teacher and one of the leaders in community drama in our area, put his hand on my shoulder the night we heard about LeRoy. "Rand, I've been listening to you. Guess what? You just got yourself a part."

Someone else was gotten to play my bit part, and I started studying the slave's lines in earnest.

We had a private, invited audience the first night. My black makeup was so realistic that when a playwright and his wife came backstage to congratulate us and I took off my shirt, his wife shrieked her astonishment at seeing I was actually white.

The makeup was as difficult to remove as it was realistic, taking more than an hour in the shower. After one of the dress rehearsals, the cast wanted to stop at a cafe for some refreshments. I looked at one of the guys, then down at my still black hand. I shrugged and went with them.

A few minutes later, we walked into that cafe — a place I'd gone countless times before. The manager knew me by my first name. In fact, I'd done him a favor. Tonight, he didn't recognize me. He walked over. "Just a minute, sir," he said. "I . . . ahem, er, well, I'd prefer that you didn't patronize this restaurant."

"You . . . *what?*"

"I would prefer you didn't . . ."

I put up my hand. My black hand. "Okay, okay. I heard you."

He tried to smile. "Nothing personal, you understand."

"Then — then what the hell *is* it?" I managed to say. I was shaking, and my teeth started grinding so I could hardly talk. I suddenly knew how it felt to be black. "You stupid, stupid . . ."

Underneath all my sudden anger and hate was a great sadness as subconsciously I realized the innate cruelty of people who make scapegoats out of those weaker than themselves. "I'd prefer that you didn't patronize...!" Not even the guts to come out with it and say, "Get the hell out of here, you inferior black bastard."

I stumbled out of that miserable place disguised so craftily as a nice, clean, respectable business establishment.

All my conscious life I had heard vague mention of Denver's ghetto. Denver? A western town? Oh, compared with ghettos in more infamous cities, it wasn't very notable. Except to the people who lived there.

In blackface one night, still feeling low about my experience, I went down to see this ghetto — to Five Points. It's a place you sometimes drove through on a Sunday afternoon with the doors locked and the windows rolled up.

I found real people, real families, that night. In the darkness, I didn't notice the color of skins. I felt at home. I talked to a lot of people. They didn't see through my mask. One black brother wanted to tell me about Jesus. I listened, chuckled, patted him on the back. In a little bar, I jived with a bunch of blacks for a while. We were all human beings together.

Another job I got during high school was in a drugstore where eventually I became an apprentice pharmacist. I learned a lot about people, about retailing, and about medicine. I learned how to deal with the public, how to display merchandise, and how to keep up the paperwork. I learned about balancing the cash register and something about profit and loss.

After a few months on the job, I had a chance to take advantage of a wartime statute still on the books in Colorado. This made it possible to combat the manpower shortage by apprenticing pharmacists at the age of 16. If you stayed on as an apprentice for seven or eight years, passed a State board examination, you could become a registered pharmacist without going to college.

I applied and became an apprentice. Then I was able to fill prescriptions — and learned a lot of interesting facts about people of the community, who was hooked on what, who had VD . . . and which doctors were alcoholics or would make out prescriptions of a quasi-legal nature. A prim and proper girl in the social set came in periodically for a sexually related drug and a high school teacher was hooked on cough syrup. I got quite an education.

One of our steady customers was Floyd Haskell, senior Senator from Colorado. It was Mom and the girls, however, who ran up the bills. Their four daughters were always at the cosmetic counter and I became expert in prescribing makeup.

In the drugstore, I had access to speed. I tried some. At first I used it to keep going when I had a lot of studying or wanted to make it dynamic on an all-night date. I would lift a pill here, a pill there.

For quite a while I turned down marijuana. I didn't think I ever wanted to smoke it. I knew my brother, Wayne, was into it. He had made it to Vietnam, and it was common knowledge how plentiful it was there. Then a customer came up to me and asked if I'd sell some grass. Naturally, I shrugged and told him I didn't carry the stuff. Somehow, though, his question startled me, and maybe flattered me. The guy was so nonchalant about it. He acted as though there was nothing wrong with it, and he obviously didn't feel guilty asking me.

Now I took a good look around me. As soon as I had something to look for, I found it, indeed. Half the high school seemed to be turning on. A guy with a locker right next to mine used it like a girl uses a vanity nook — to sneak a couple of puffs with his head out of sight among his books. I discovered Colorado was a dope smokers' paradise. Tons of hashish was readily available. I decided to join the 'in' crowd.

I started on grass. After half a dozen joints, I began to wonder what it was all about. Nothing happened. I tried some more. Still, nothing. I began to get frightened. Was I abnormal, or something?

The tenth time, I was with a bunch of guys and girls in somebody's basement rumpus room. After a few minutes the conversation showed that everyone was beginning to turn on, lose their inhibitions, feel with it. Everyone except me. I looked from funny face to funny face and grunted. I got off the floor where I had been sitting and said, "I've had it, people. I don't feel it, and it's obvious I'm not going to. Either you guys are a bunch of fakes or your constitution is different. So long. Have a good time."

"Yeah, yeah, man," was all I heard as I went up the stairs.

"Hi, Dad, Hi, Mom," I flipped over my shoulder mechanically as I swept through the house to my room. In bed, I lay with my arms under my head feeling as though as I had been cheated. Puff the Magic Dragon was for kids after all. The trip scene was just dramatics and I for one thought it was bad theater. I'd show them I vowed, I'd go to the barber's. Tomorrow . . .

Outside the crickets were cricketing . . . louder. And louder. And then I could see them. And they were getting bigger. And bigger. And pretty soon, they were the size of dragons. Magic dragons.

The chirping echoed in my head. My bed seemed like rubber underneath, a trampoline. My legs started to grow. They stretched . . . clear around the world . . . and came back from the other direction to kick at my hair.

I jumped up excitedly. "This is it!" I had to get out of the house! I made it out, got on my bike and within minutes I was back at the party.

They could tell I had finally switched on. But they didn't

show much expression . . . they looked like vegetables sitting there on the floor in the blue haze, each living inwardly some "delightful" experience they would not remember later. After that, I took a few trips now and then, about once or twice a month. It was still rather scary. Smoking grass was illegal and decidedly disapproved of by grown-ups. At this point, I still cared a little about such things as reputation and social approval. Except, sometimes, when the rock beat got heavy, and flesh was flaming and lights flashed. . .

During the summer of 1966, between my sophomore and junior year at high school, I got a part in the interscholastic drama program's production of *Kiss Me Kate,* singing the gangster's "Brush Up Your Shakespeare." It was in this play that I met Ed Kane. The day I met Ed, he had just crashed his Volkswagen in the parking lot of a car dealer. We became instant friends.

Kiss Me Kate was one of the high points in my early dramatic training. The Beatles' "Magical Mysteries" and the Buffalo Springfield song, "For What It's Worth," had just come out. My mind was on music. It was the first time I'd had a chance to sing on stage in a musical with full orchestra.

Mr. Oden and some other teachers were investigating several study-abroad programs, with the aim of taking a group of students the following year to Europe. Mr. Oden agreed to include me in the select group which would enroll in whatever program was chosen for students in our area. This turned out to be the American Study Program sponsored by the Institute for Intramural Studies at the University of Southampton, England. The program was offering college level courses for six weeks.

"You'll have to raise around $800," Mr. Oden told me. I knew I'd be working at the drugstore for another year. Going to England and France was something that appealed to me, and the chance to include some dramatics in the studies abroad was the clincher. The list would include four boys and ten girls, along with Mr. Oden and his wife. Ed Kane would be one of us.

Meanwhile, when the school year started, I developed an interest I had started in my sophomore year, journalism. I had concentrated on photo journalism and worked for the school newspaper as well as the yearbook. I'd become skillful in book and magazine layout, and I was promised the position of editor of the yearbook the following year. But all I anticipated on the horizon was the chance to fly free and high over ocean and land in a fascinating world that stretched endlessly back in time.

5

ENGLAND! Ed acted blase, but I could tell that he, too, was awed by the thought that we were visiting a country that had first had its beginnings around the sixth century. King Alfred had had a rough row to hoe, doing his bit to unite the country, but traditions started then were still respected today. We could see signs of these traditions at the University of Southampton, where we studied — traditions of pageantry and color that preserved the form of an ancient world.

Ed and I quickly got used to Guiness Stout. We liked the English girls, too. We loved to hear them talk, and we were put straight in a hurry about one difference in customs between America and England: in England, you court and court and court a girl. You don't kiss her on the first date. Later, if she decides to let you kiss her, you can pretty well assume that she is saying "yes" to more intimate pleasures.

By the time the six weeks in England were over, Ed and I had made many friends and had developed such a love for the country, with all its bloody past, that I was loathe to leave.

The friends we had made, the new but old country we had seen, made us realize that America wasn't always right.

After we were all packed and ready to go by boat across

the English Channel to Le Havre, France, for our last week of tour, we pushed ourselves over to the friendly local pub the night before departure.

Trying to drown our real feelings in alcohol, we had countless gin and tonics, singing and talking until they closed the place, not wanting to say those final goodbyes. The next morning, they almost had to pour us onto the boat.

But you can't stay down very long when you're on your way to Paris. In between our touring of the City of Light, we sat at a table on the Left Bank drinking *cafe noir* and watching people. Here there seemed no generation gap. We were accepted everywhere, shown what to see, where to stay, and how to spend our money. The old and the new, the young and the ancient, existed harmoniously side-by-side. There seemed to be a smoother flowing of the river of time. I felt in touch with my surroundings, a part of it — not a frantic organism cut off and anxious.

It seemed to me that here everyone started out and developed with the same frame of reference and in an orderly, step-by-step process. They did not suddenly jump from one stage of life to the other, suddenly acquire the status, say, of teenager, with a whole new set of rules and procedures and fashions and language to learn all over again. And the pace was so much slower.

All too soon our seven days were over. We boarded a student-packed jetliner that was to take us to New York in seven hours. I was anxious to see New York again. We'd just touched the city briefly on our way to England. "That's my city," I told Ed. "Everybody calls it a jungle, but I bet I can handle it. Want to come to New York with me, after we graduate?"

Ed hesitated, then replied, "I don't know. I like Denver."

Now, after seeing England and falling in love with it completely, I wasn't sure, either. But we didn't have time to see New York again. It was raining hard when we landed at JFK Airport, and we had to board the plane for Denver

IT'S GOOD TO KNOW 29

almost immediately. But as it turned out the plane had all kinds of mechanical difficulties, and we didn't arrive at Denver until 4:30 a.m. I thought Mom and Dad would bombard me with questions, but they were so tired from waiting and worrying, they hardly asked anything. School friends, I thought. The yearbook kids. Wait'll they hear about it!

The next morning, I went to school, still tired from thirty hours travel time. I was anxious to get to work on the yearbook. It was hard to believe this was the beginning of my senior year.

As I headed for my locker, the Principal called out, 'Wait a minute, Randy.'' He caught up, "Ahh, Randy, there have been a few changes. I was showing the Superintendent around this summer. In a drawer in the darkroom, we ran across some prints you'd made — enlargements. They're not very nice pictures.''

I thought back, then it hit me. I'd gotten hold of some frames from a movie, showing an artist chasing a model around a room in their underwear, but nothing really revealing. The girl had a bra on and it was funnier than it was "dirty," nowhere near as provocative as *Playboy* at the corner drugstore.

"You realize the Superintendent, the president of the school board, and a few other people saw those. We've decided to appoint someone else editor of the yearbook.''

"But, sir!" I was shaking. "I already have it half-laid out. All planned. I've got some real neat ideas. . .''

"Randy," he cut me off. "You don't seem to realize the seriousness of what you've done. We just can't have that going on here. The editorship of the yearbook is a very important post, we have to have someone on whom we can rely implicitly. Someone we can trust. . .''

"Yes, sir," I muttered softly.

"I'll change your schedule and substitute seventh-period study hall.''

"Study hall?" I exploded. "With all those goof-offs who can't get their work done, throwing paper airplanes around and mouthing off?"

"Simmer down, Randy. You should have thought about the consequences of using school equipment and materials that way. It's too late."

I must have looked totally dejected for after awhile he sighed, "Listen, Randy, this doesn't mean you can't take pictures for the newspaper and yearbook, like you used to. You can even use the darkroom. You can still participate. We'll give you that much of a chance, so don't feel like it's the end of the world."

End of the world! I'd just come back from seeing more of the world than most of the jocks in that school, even the teachers, ever had. Something in me seemed to snap. It was almost as if all that uplifting experience I'd had overseas hadn't even happened.

Unprintable words flashed red. Had I really had that beautiful experience just a few short days ago? Or had it been a dream? What had it accomplished? A small world, after all. A damned, small, small world!

The darkroom . . . it was like being on a trip in my own head — total blackness except for the eerie wash of reddened darkness from a small bulb in the ceiling. A blackness both restful and frightening. After a while, the blackness seemed to move in waves. I was staggered by the nothingness of it. And from the lack of sound — a blackness of sound, too.

By squinching my eyes, I could discern the dim, rectangular form of a pinkish tray on an unseen counter. When I bent still closer and stared, I could see what was in the bottom, swimming in the dark waters, materializing before my eyes. It was a photo of the Principal, standing as he spoke recently at a Rotary luncheon, snapped by one of

IT'S GOOD TO KNOW 31

the journalism students for our school paper. Only it wasn't.

"Okay," my dark being spat, "you said those photos I developed were 'pornographic,' because by your piggish double standard, little, innocent, baby high school students aren't supposed to know anything about them. Well, if you thought those pictures were shocking, how about this?"

In my mind's eye, I ripped the clothes off the Principal and all the Rotarians and their straight wives sitting beside them and imagined the most grotesque features and contortions I could dredge up from the deepest, vilest, blackest pits of imagination. "There, you straight pigs!" I thought. "That's how you really look!"

The darkroom became my refuge. And my hell. It was the only place during the week where I could get away from the confusion of other people and be quietly and profoundly alone. Sometimes, as I waited for negatives and prints to develop, I reflected on what I thought about life, and what I should think about it. Out of the darkness would come images and voices and ideas — transitory, ephemeral, but disturbing. . .

I further developed my concept of morality. Already being into sex, I thought it was a holier-than-thou impudence of "them" to try to legislate ecstasy. Sex was ecstasy. So why the big deal about it? To me morality was not letting down someone who needs help.

And what did the length of my hair have to do with anything? Why did my Dad, most of the faculty and administration, and the church people make such a big issue over it? The more they complained about my long hair, the more determined I was to keep it long. I felt they were attacking my freedom.

It was a lousy way to start out my senior year. I'd come back from an inspiring experience, learning about people of other countries, seeing great scenes of the past and scenes of living history, to a slap in the face, this tug at the hair, this lock-step conformity. In England, I thought, I had caught a glimpse of what civilization could be like. . .

There was one other class besides honors English (which Mr. Oden had arranged for me to take in place of seventh-period study hall) where a teacher seemed to have a larger view. And that teacher taught a class in civilization — "Contemporary Civilization." He had come to Littleton High School the previous year, after teaching the children of American engineers and others employed by a big oil company on the Persian Gulf for several years. His vivid descriptions of that land, classic cradle of civilization, lent great authenticity to his presentation of modern history. He was criticized by some for "left-wing leanings." I thought his lectures were tremendous.

His ideas appealed to Ed, Doug, and me, and whether it was intentional or not, topics he brought up stimulated much thinking and directed our attention in sharper focus to subjects which concerned me greatly. My brother's return from Vietnam the previous spring, and the few things he said about some of his experiences and observations there, made me think a whole lot about the war and what it meant, or didn't mean.

I eagerly looked forward to the next presidential election. Some said that Bobby Kennedy had a good chance to get the nomination. A ray of hope. . .

It seemed as though the Vietnam war had been going on for centuries. When I was in the darkroom, I seemed to see the vicious aggression in human beings spilling out in blood. The water in the developing trays seemed to be blood, spilling senselessly because of a few fat, generals and rich industrialists. Blood of innocent victims used to develop profits and enlarge empires. Sometimes in that darkroom, when images of carnage flashed in the eerie red light, I would feel cold, stiff. Dead.

Outside, I tried to talk to people about the crime of Vietnam and of the whole economic set-up that perpetrated it and kept it going and going and going. Nobody wanted to

IT'S GOOD TO KNOW

listen. So many straights were ranting about God and Country, waving the flag, as if to excuse their bloody crimes, plastering bumper stickers on their cars — AMERICA! LOVE IT OR LEAVE IT! How I wished that the silent majority would shut up!

My darkroom became even more a place of retreat, that warm fall of '67, as hippies lolled on the grass during lunchtime, fondling dandelions, smiling sweetly, murmuring quietly, and humming serenely about love, love, love and occasionally bend a joint in the shelter of a bush. They had the answer. Love was the answer to the world's problems.

Even on our high school stage came a reminder of the oppression of the Establishment. I won a part in the play, *The Madwoman of Chaillot* by Jean Giradoux. The setting was present-day Paris, and the theme was rampant industrialism threatening to deface this ancient city of marvels — and the weird reprisal taken by the "mad" woman who sent members of the Establishment down a one-way stairway into "hell."

Between honors English, and Mr. Oden and the drama department, my senior year was rescued from being a complete fizzle. The play was the thing that kept Humpty Dumpty together until Christmas vacation of 1967.

A few days before school resumed again I had a chance to get some Purple Ozley Eight Ways — LSD! This particular kind would do eight people on one hit.

I had intentionally kept away from LSD. People said how dangerous it was, how it could affect the genes of your descendants. I told the guy who offered the Ozleys to me, "No thanks!"

He said, "Well, if you change your mind..."

I decided to take a short trip to Boulder, thinking maybe a change of scenery would make me feel better. I had diagnosed the world's problems and still prescribed love as the treatment. I was still a hippie — peace and love was the antidote I offered. Flower power was the thing. Smile and give people flowers; they would flip.

I wanted love, but I couldn't get it from the Establishment. Its love was conditional. "I'll love you — if you get a haircut. If you do this, if you do that. . ." So I tried to find love among the hippies. I sold grass to them, they gave me love. I listened to their songs, they gave me love.

The flower children told me they had all the love I'd ever need. "When the chips are down," they said, "we'll be there."

But hitchhiking home from Boulder in ice cold weather, a few days before the end of Christmas vacation, a car came by, a warm car with an empty seat in the back. I was standing in the blizzard. The car was full of hippies . . . long-hairs . . . my super-loving friends. I recognized a couple I'd sold dope to in Boulder.

They drove right by. As they passed, a cute little hippie girl in the rear seat pointed at me, smiled, and gave me the peace sign.

"You can have your peace, baby," I yelled after them. "If that's peace, I'll take war. If that's love, I'll take hate." So what else is new? Man's inhumanity to man — the oldest theme there is. "I love you, but I won't give you a ride in the snowstorm . . . I love you — as long as you've got dope."

In what way were the hippies different from the old folks? The hippies said sweet words of love and listened to their rock-and-roll stars and begged and stole money to buy millions of dollars worth of their records, thinking their stars were gods and goddesses, yet didn't believe a word of it.

So, when I got back to Denver, I dropped acid — 2½ tabs of 8-ways. I felt it coming on immediately. After a while, I began to "peak." I was way out, tripped-out completely. The peak lasted six or eight hours.

LSD makes everything dramatic, makes you super-sensitive. All the complaints I had — the imagined oppressions and the real shortcomings of society — were magnified. I could *see* pollution: cars, airplanes became billowed large and small, as though they were breathing . . . I could see people's breath, see the dirty air. Factories looked like monsters about to eat me up. The South Platte River was a solid movement of crud . . . it rose like a tidal wave to devour me.

I began to hate my father and his generation. To his generation, my life wasn't worth two-bits, I felt. If that was the case, their lives weren't worth two-bits to me. If someone was going to try to take my life, maybe I'd better be ready to take his first.

If I'm not part of the solution, a small cry against war and hate and destruction of natural resources, then I'm part of the pollution, I thought, and I might as well be dead. LSD changed me from a pot-smoking, hippie-loving, love-happy flower child to a real radical — a yippie.

At the peak of the LSD experience, I saw the typical blinding white light that blotted out everything — except the non-visual concepts, the flashing, distorted visions manufactured eerily out of reality.

Trillions of bits of stimulus made me super-sensitive to the dimmest, most fleeting sounds and to my own feeblest whispers, my pulse and glandular secretions. The white light itself had a sound that battered my eardrums, pulsed in my head. I felt as though I was tuning in on others' thoughts and it was horrible, what the world was thinking. At the same time I felt Godlike and omniscient. Yet at the same time powerless.

The white was so bright and blinding, it seemed almost to be black, and the same kinds of feelings I'd had in the darkroom, only infinitely more intense, assailed me.

In the wake of this came laughter. Suddenly, everything was outrageously hilarious. I rocked with howls of merriment. The galaxy was a huge joke, and the stars composing it mere vibrations in a sea of laughing gas all around.

When I came out of it, I was sobered. What tremendous

powers had I casually allowed to take control over me?

I felt very young and inexperienced to have been under such a frightening influence.

When school started, I determined to try to stay with it until graduation, in late May. I tried to block out increasing anger at contradictions in society, contradictions to which LSD had sensitized me.

I tried to ignore remarks about long hair and the examples of the double standard I saw all around me.

I tried not to see around me the hate, and the violence supressed or expressed, and the anxiety furrowing once-handsome, once-young faces. I tried not to see the problems, problems, problems that hammered and bonged and rattled all around me.

I struggled through the school year, tempted to take another trip, and then was immediately horrified at the thought. I felt weak inside, as though I had little resistance to whatever influence might try to get at me.

The two sides of me were polarized, pulling me in opposite directions. The least pressure from one side or the other, and I'd fly apart.

Then, at last, graduation! I was free.

Free? Well, anyway, I was out of high school.

My graduation present was something to lift my spirits, a real surprise. I'd be in the air again, like a bird! I was given a flight to San Francisco to see Wayne. He and I would drive back to Colorado together.

In San Francisco I got a taste of Haight-Ashbury, chased girls, followed hippies and bought rings, hippie beads, and marijuana. And Wayne and I drove back.

Along the way, Wayne told me what it was like in Vietnam. But he said things looked hopeful. It looked like the upcoming presidential election offered a good chance for

IT'S GOOD TO KNOW

a real change. He, Wayne, the guy who'd actually been there, who'd seen it all, was trying to cheer *me* up!

It might have helped me. Except shortly after we got home, we got the news over the TV, from the Ambassador Hotel in Los Angeles, June 5, 1968 . . . Bobby Kennedy had been shot!

6

I WAS ALL ALONE — alone in the darkness of an abandoned mine shaft in the mountains, sitting on a mossy rock in a small chamber once used as a turn-around point for carts laden with gold-bearing ore.

I was beat from cleaning cabins, bussing dishes and helping in the kitchen at the Peak Inn, one of numerous tourist resorts in Central City, not far west of Denver. It was a quaint alpine town, sleeping in a wistful reminiscence of gold and good times.

I'd come to Central City to work for the summer and to be alone, away from people I knew. I wanted to put everything together. Everything was up for review.

Twelve years of schooling had ended. I was at the bottom of a long ladder leading upward, its top out of sight . . . the ladder leading into adult life. I needed to set some directions for myself.

I felt I had lost so much in the past few years.

I felt empty, as empty as the musty, rotting mine, long since robbed of its treasures.

I felt robbed.

But why? Why did I feel this way?

Who had robbed me?

They, a voice in the shadows answered. The Establishment pigs. The fat, rich people who make a profit out of everyone else's troubles. Your father. . .

I shook my head. I didn't want to believe that. My father had worked hard all his life to provide for his family. We always had plenty to eat. A decent house. Good clothes. Extra money for fun.

My parents tried to be loving. They invited me places. Sometimes, I couldn't go. They were reluctant sometimes for me to be with them because of the way I looked and behaved. My long hair bugged them.

Tears came to my eyes. I punched my palm with my fist. Why should long hair make such a difference?

I shook my head again. How could I be sure who was responsible for all the problems in the world? How could I blame my father for all the world's problems? How could I blame any one person? Or one group more than the others? How had the hippies done any better? They lied, stole, let their babies go naked and dirty, loafed, tripped out. They talk about love but all they really meant was sex.

Suddenly, the darkness was too much for me. I hurried up the shaft, stumbling, afraid, bumping against timbers, dirt showering down on me. My heart raced. What if I caused a cave-in?

Then I grunted. What the hell if I did? What would it matter, anyway? I was dead already.

All I wanted to do that summer was tune in, turn on, and drop out. But I had to go to college, to be exempt from the draft. So, I enrolled in the University of Colorado at Boulder. At least, it was an active social school. And wild. Right away, I got three different parts in the same play, *Waiting for Lefty,* by Clifford Odets, and after that, I got a part in *Marat/Sade.*

By now, I was weird enough to fit right in. The setting was an insane asylum in France before the French revolution.

Some of the inmates were there for drunkeness or for simply being non-conformists.

Our director, Mrs. Carol Olin, was anxious to make this play as authentic as possible and teach us the importance of thoroughly understanding the situations and roles. She organized a research program which included the showing of "restricted" medical films featuring deranged people and what goes on inside mental institutions.

Around this time, I was weighing the pros and cons of going on another "trip." Timothy Leary's proclamations that you can take yourself to plateaus of consciousness, find real love, discover knowledge and insight, and become tuned into the universe, sounded great. And the high I'd gotten from my first trip just after Christmas had had its moments. But the overall effect of the trip had been uncomfortable. I'd felt as though I had surrendered control to a power whose designs could not be fathomed.

"Still, why not?" I would think the next moment. Anyone who can do better with this body, be my guest.

A lot of things were flashing through my mind at this time. I'd seen the movie *2001,* and the idea of following a radio beam and being sucked into the eye of Japetas (one of Jupiter's moons), or negative space, and being reborn as a star-child with God-like control, fascinated me.

2001 was, for me, kind of a testimonial that there was other intelligence in the universe. We were not alone. There were others to save us besides God.

I'd had to revisit Littleton High to get some records for the college admissions office and had been startled at being challenged in the hallway by an armed guard, who had to clear me with the administration office. This was the school from which I'd graduated! Police on duty. Incredible! "Dope's rampant here, Rand, since you left," the school secretary explained. "We had a 'Romeo and Juliet death.' They say they were high on drugs. Everyone's really frightened about the dope problem here. They even have locker checks."

Then there were the kooks of the funny farm. Our drama director, Mrs. Olin, must have had friends in the University's psychology department and they, in turn, must have had some leverage with the State Mental Hospital because we were allowed several hours to wander around through the wards and talk to people.

The director of the play was standing with several members of the cast at the wide entrance to a huge, tiled room bursting with patients in hospital pajamas. The lucky minority sat on the chairs and benches or at the few tables scattered throughout, a few reading or playing cards, the vast majority sitting on the floor, some of them motionless, out of it completely.

A TV screen flashed up near the ceiling and dozens of eyes were aimed at it but no one could have heard it. The restless inmates made it too noisy even to think.

"That's what you call mass insanity," our director sighed. "It's their dayroom. Supposedly where they come to relax. You can see it's slightly over-crowded." She paused to let that choice revelation stew for a moment. "They have a building program but it doesn't keep up. Admissions to mental institutions in the U.S. have doubled in fifteen years."

An intern guiding us through remarked, "You know how much they spend a year on mental hospitals? A paltry $2 billion. That's only a little over $4,600 a year per inmate. Try to buy room, board, laundry, the works, and constant supervision and even a little bit of medical attention for that anywhere else."

One of our guys said, "How does that grab you? Our defense department spent $80 billion last year."

During our visit, we saw catatonics — people so

completely withdrawn, they had to be fed by hand and carried to bed. We saw the violent ones behind heavy glass doors, guys that had to be put into strait-jackets when it was their turn to go in for shock therapy or to see the doctor.

There was a veteran of the Korean War who was temporarily here for some special treatment the V.A. hospital couldn't provide. And a guy who muggers had castrated. And dozens of drug users and a couple of cops.

All the time I was there, I was shaky. It gave me a creepy feeling, like I recognized . . . someone.

What did it mean, anyway, all these human wrecks packed away in such a place? Why were they there? What had happened to them?

During the early phases of learning our lines for *Marat/Sade,* the cast would sit on stage and rap. I was telling about my feelings from seeing the movie *2001.* "It's pretty groovy thinking about starting to get out into space. Maybe there is something in the Eye of Japetas. . ."

"Yeah, but what about this, Randy? They spend all that bread and learn how to get man out into space, and spend all that energy in war weapons, missiles, and all that junk. But still we're in the dark ages when it comes to living with each other."

"Yeah, that's stupid, man" I answered. "I feel like I should just turn on. The bit."

"Why not?"

Then I said with emotion, "I tripped. Once. But everyone says it's bad on the genes. Then, in the kook house, they say a lot of them are in there because of drugs."

"They've really got you suckered, man. Maybe some of those guys were on acid. The real reason they're in there is that the pigs want to keep them out of circulation. They've seen too much. Like Leary said, they dropped a few times and saw the light. Those bastard pigs are scared to let them out loose. They'll tell too much."

"You might be right on, except that I talked to some of them, and they really were nutty," I said.

"With a few volts of shock therapy and a few slices with the surgeon's knife . . . you know, lobotomy? They can create Frankensteins easy. No problem. Then they have a perfect excuse to keep them like vegetables in a deep freeze. Permanently."

Suddenly, it made sense to me: it was a conspiracy! I felt a sudden thrill. I could trip and not feel guilty, or worry about it! I could get that beautiful light again and soak in all those perceptions, and talk mind-to-mind with my buddies. It was music to my ears, what I'd been wanting to hear! All that stuff I'd heard against dope was just brainwashing.

And it was probably made up, that story about the Littleton High School boy and girl who'd died. Was there any proof they'd been on dope? It was just an excuse to put cops in the school and keep the kids from turning on. The Establishment knew if kids really got with it, they'd see through all the lies the military and industrialist pigs use to keep us slaving for them. That they had to have cops on the campus was actually a sign of victory. It showed young people were waking up! It was their last-ditch act of desperation. The death throes of a dying system.

As soon as I could get hold of some acid, I'd trip! Meanwhile, on with the play. I really dug it! It was the ultimate in protest plays.

I played Polpoch, one of the singers. The singers were rounders, rogues, who had been tossed into the asylum for drunkenness and debauchery. In the institution, they continued playing cards, singing loudly, fighting with one another, generally distracting the more serious inmates, who were looking to Marat, to lead them to revolution. Here were inmates wailing about the injustices of society, especially how the poor were being kept poor. The play was crazy, wild and inflamatory, and it knocked the sense out of me.

We had an invited audience for the first dress rehearsal. I had just gotten some LSD, and I thought it would be a great idea to have six of my friends come to the rehearsal for the last scene. They didn't know what the play was about; I thought it would be a gas to surprise them.

"We'll all drop at the same time," I told them. "Just before the final curtain. Be sure to synchronize your watches. It'll take just about the right amount of time for the acid to come on just as the play is over. It'll be a gas."

A few minutes before the last curtain, I swallowed a cap. The last scene was a chaos of inmates breaking loose and going on a rampage, right out into the audience. According to our timing, my friends would walk in for that last scene, the acid still dormant. They would be amused, we'd walk out and get together at someone's pad, and let the LSD come on with that last scene in the background — but not too soon to cause any straights around to know about our trip, or to freak us out too much.

It didn't work that way; the trip came on more quickly. I was on the stage, and suddenly I felt slightly spaced out. I tried to tell myself I was just imagining it. I saw my friends walk in. The inmates started crawling off the stage just as my friends turned on, heightening the spectacle, as even the most trivial things are magnified on an acid trip. They didn't need dozens of snarling, spitting, foaming-at-the-mouth, grotesquely made-up lunatics slithering off the stage right into the audience, pursued by male nurses with clubs who "bash" them to "death."

My acid friends were wiped out — several of them shrieked themselves right into a bummer. I couldn't really console them, because I had a big, eight-inch scar painted across my face and looked like hell personsified.

We did get outside, although the director, Mrs. Olin, sensing that my friends were far more startled than what

IT'S GOOD TO KNOW

was to be expected, gave me a look that chilled me.

Another prank backfiring . . . luckily not sending one of my friends out into the street, in front of a truck or something. I had had a lot more luck than I should have had up to now.

When my parents phoned saying they'd like to come for the official opening, I felt really uptight. This was one play I would have preferred they didn't see me in. I was afraid they wouldn't understand.

From their expressions — grim mouths, noble attempts to congratulate me on first night — I could tell I had anticipated correctly. Mom timidly said, "Wasn't that rather radical? You don't believe all that, do you?"

I shrugged. "Mother, it's just a play. I'm an actor." I hoped she would understand.

She didn't.

Who did?

A couple of weeks earlier, on that acid trip, I had cursed my parents as members of a hated generation, a generation which had made this stinking world for me and refused to do anything to change it.

Well, if they wouldn't help me, LSD would. I felt as though LSD was an ally, giving me cosmic, Godlike powers, making me a sorcerer's apprentice who could consider that because the Establishment had refused to listen, he would be justified in blowing up banks, burning cities, even killing — even killing his parents. Overthrowing the regime, killing their system.

And LSD would see me through all this. As the musical group Blood Sweat and Tears sang in "Smiling Faces."

"Keep on smiling through and through
And you'll be amazed at the gazes
On their faces as they sentence you."

If I couldn't communicate with the "older" generation, at least I could communicate with cosmic powers of the universe and with other guys on LSD. I found acid made it even more difficult to communicate with straights. It was difficult to order food in a restaurant, for the waitress and me to understand each other, when I was high. But others on a trip with me could understand, without even verbalizing. I'd get this idea of violence, and they'd sense it without saying anything. Or so it seemed. A look, a shudder, a thought wave...

I couldn't communicate with my own parents, but when I was on acid, I could talk to dogs! "Hello, dog, how are you?" And the dog would answer back.

The trip's real appeal was the high it wrought, the riotous laughter and swinging good time and ecstatic feelings, the guiltless abandon into pure self-centeredness. A word from a fellow tripper would trigger hysterics. It was madness, frivolity — at the expense of anyone and everyone. It was "me first" and the rest of the universe be damned. That was our version of Leary's cosmic system!

Considering the horror stories I'd heard of others on acid trips, and some I'd seen with my own eyes, I was lucky in having a good trip — good for me, that is.

Not so good for regular, everyday people who had to put up with me and my crowd, but to hell with them. They perpetuated this sorry mess of pollution, blood-letting and fear.

I did have after-effects, though none of the searing flashbacks, I'd heard about. Three days after one trip, I saw things jump, like a tree when there wasn't any wind. And I saw clouds flashing on and off. A car following itself. I felt a rush of blood, a buzzing starting from my toes, going clear through my body, soul, and mind, and out of the top of my head. But that was all. For me, a trip was mostly pure pleasure.

That trip hyped me up so that I dropped all fears and doubts and became a staunch-out freak in the drug culture. Man, I would have all the joys of my new cosmic real estate of the mind, including the bread part of it. It was too good a deal to pass up, to be able to lead others to the salvation of the higher cosmic powers while at the same time raking in loot. I decided I would push.

7

MY ENTRY into the drug trade took an unusual twist, as I became a retail merchandiser in the mail-order business. I got a kick out of the fact that the U.S. Post Office was working with me as a silent partner and respected the silent part of it by never breathing a word to them how much they were helping me.

What happened was I discovered the address of a place in New York State, and another in California, that would mail acid. Postpaid, of course. No C.O.D.'s or checks.

One variety of LSD sent this way was called "blotter acid." Another, "window panes." In the former, small drops of LSD were dropped in rows on blotter paper sheets the size of business-size envelopes. The receiver merely had to cut out a drop, which was just barely visible to the naked eye. You put the tiny square of acid-soaked blotter on your tongue.

Window pane acid came in sheets of digestible celluloid. You clipped off these brown or purple dots and swallowed them like mini-wafers. In the blotter acid, sheets usually came with five rows of 20 "hits" each and sometimes I'd make a sale which involved ordering 20 sheets in one envelope.

I wanted to be fair and businesslike about it. My drug

IT'S GOOD TO KNOW

store merchandising training paid off in giving me a figure for the mark-up — one-third profit to myself. By participating in the distribution phase of the drug culture in this way, I felt useful and involved, as though there was some meaning in life. My life. I was quite successful.

One time, one of those acid letters had an interesting interlude in the Post Office. It got jammed in the canceling machine and the envelope was destroyed. The Post Office carefully stapled the blotters to steno paper and sent them on to me in a government envelope with a polite apology to the effect that, despite eternal vigilence, one out of every trillion pieces of mail got gummed up in the works. "We are constantly trying to improve our service, and hope that you will bear with our occasional failures." There had been several thousand dollars worth of LSD in that envelope.

What was really ironic was how I sold the stuff once I got it. It was the campus bus run that put me in the ideal position to distribute so profitably those little paper passports to the infinite.

And I got some pin money from the university bursar's office for driving a bus, to boot. What I'd done was answer an ad in the school newspaper — WANTED: BUS DRIVER. MUST BE NON-DRINKER (etc., etc.). I got the job.

I was trusted with the keys, so I had my pick of buses. We would make arrangements like, "I need 2,000 whites by Friday. I'll have the money."

"Right, pal," I would answer, "be at Stop No. 2."

Some runs were really just one big trip, ending up in the mountains with a whole bus-load of students stoned and happy. Incredibly, such little joy rides were never discovered. The run to Williams Village each morning and back again in the afternoon was the best dope drop in town and not much chance of a rip-off. We were dealing in small amounts per student, but it added up into the hundreds fast.

One Sunday morning I headed for the usual church run. One student got off, and while I was waiting for someone else to board, I was so hung over from dope I fell asleep. Since no one showed up, I slept for three hours until someone shook me. "Randy, Randy. Wake up. Your motor's still running. Randy . . . you fell asleep." It was my boss.

"Uh? Oh, yeh, sure. I'll finish the run."

"You're a bit late. There are some unhappy people down at the Village. They missed Sunday School. You were due there three hours ago."

I used my winning smile and the boss, not knowing what was going on, forgave and forgot.

I was beginning to freak out of my classes with a big F, and I needed this job to fill in my time and for money. Money for booze, dope, girls, rags, and gas for our chariot.

I could never get enough play-acting. For kicks sometimes I would go around in blackface. I figured if I was in the right setting at the right time, those holier-than-thou sorority queens who tried to show how liberal they were by going out with black men might give me a tumble.

For laughs once, I picked up one of those girls. Her place was in a high-class neighborhood of old, old houses. The kind that, because they were so big and hard to keep up, had been partitioned off into basement-to-attic cubicles, mislabeled apartments.

It was midnight when we got there, but there were gals and guys milling all over, in a haze of blue smoke, which reminded me I hadn't had a joint for a while. "Got any grass?" I asked as we headed for the second-floor landing.

She turned around and hollered down to one of the girls just going by the stairway, calling loudly enough to let everyone know that she, a white girl, was making it with a black.

I hoped she had an attic pad, where lots of guys and gals just lie stoned for days looking up through the skylight at the moon and stars, then watching the whole world as it flashed by during the day. But, no, she had a cramped den on the second. She shut the door, but I noticed as she started to strip that she didn't lock the door or turn out the lights.

"Huh, uh. No lights, baby," I said. I had to have it that way, or she'd see that I was black only on my face and lower arms. I had to tense my muscles to keep from laughing at the thought of her thinking she was making it with a black man.

After a while, I got out of bed and put my clothes back on, except my shirt so she could see my broad, white chest. Then I switched on the light. When she saw me, she gasped and choked. "What is this?" she sputtered.

"Just showing you up for the phoney you are," I said, laughing as I left.

The semester was nearing its end, and LSD had been my prof. Driving their piggy buses and playing black on the other side of the tracks now suddenly seemed stupid.

I wanted to get into some real action where maybe some heads would start rolling and buildings burning. That bit. It was a good time for it. Dissent was brewing over the imminent appearance on campus of our arch enemy, S.I. Hayakawa, who had dared to defy campus radicals at San Francisco State.

He came. During his speech, everyone was restless, moving their feet, coughing, making just enough noise to get under Hayakawa's hide. Oh, we weren't disrespectful. No, sir. No one called any names. And then the blacks did their thing, all rising at the same time, by coincidence, of course, and started walking out. One tripped over a chair. The chair scraped the floor. Someone picked it up and heaved it.

Mr. Hayakawa was ushered out fast as chairs began flying all over the place. I hadn't noticed the presence of university photographers until I was blinded by a flash of light in my face — just as I balanced a chair over my head.

My actions at the distrubance, in conjunction with my record of straight F's, won me a two-year suspension.

I kept busy that summer thinking up other ways to get back at the government for everything and for being busted out of school. By now, my draft lottery number was in favorable opposition to Mars. I no longer had to worry about trying to get back in school, and I felt released from pressure and free. I thought I might go to New York, which would take bread.

I decided to work on that, and when the Fall term started at Boulder, I drove up to see Ed, who was still hanging on. I still had all my stuff in the apartment we shared after I left the dorm, and he suggested I stay and try to get a part in a play.

I snagged two parts, that of the Archbishop in the first part and that of King Louis in the second, in *Becket*. The play was based on the Twelfth Century Anglo-French intrigues between church and State, featuring King Henry II, King Louis, and the Archbishop of Canterbury. The play brought back good memories of England.

Learning the lines of two characters was hard; for some reason (I'd never have dreamed of blaming all the LSD), I'd lost my photographic memory, but I was so impressed with Becket's one long prayer to God, a soliloquy, I learned it better than the guy playing the part. It was stupid for me to be so hung up on that prayer, because religion was just a ploy to keep people enslaved. Any time anyone talked God to me, I turned off.

The political and military themes in the play were right on. I likened the king's powers to that of the U.S. government to send us into a war we didn't want to fight, to draft us out of our time of learning, right out of our most productive years, to become cannon fodder.

While rehearsals were in full swing, some interesting things were happening in Denver at the university campus. The Vietnam war was alive and healthy, and the students,

IT'S GOOD TO KNOW 53

headed by some of the more vocal members of the Students for a Democratic Society (SDS), were beginning to flip.

A "white sheet" had been distributed to all students. We didn't know what other organization besides the SDS might be involved, but it spelled out loud and clear some of their aims. I read it aloud to Ed one night after rehearsal —

THE WHITE PAPER
Here are some ways we can help our college campus:
1. Get the President of the college or the regents into reacting angrily about some group, so they will slur the group's character. This makes an indirect slap at the entire campus.
2. Get a few of the campus respectables to go along with some of our suggestions.
3. Create a dialectic situation so the administration will be forced to reject requests that seem sensible to others. This will alienate the entire campus from the administration.
4. Support black power by any means necessary, not excluding riot, arson, and mayhem.
5. Condemn the "aggression of the U.S. Government against the people of Vietnam." This war is illegal. People haven't voted on it.
6. Fight pollution.
7. Hold more student workshops to keep them informed of goals. Goals are: basic changes, such as resignation of the President; abolition of the Board of Regents; and the addition of certain classes.
8. We have ways mapped out that will bring any uncooperative campus to a grinding halt. There are forty "target" campuses. The University of Colorado is one of them. We need your help. Join us now!

"Great, eh?" I said after I'd read it to Ed. "Just one thing; I'll go along 100 percent with this, but I'm not going to get my name on anything. That's just for suckers."

Opportunities for putting the White Paper in practice began popping up all over the place. A huge group of students and rabble-rousers stormed Denver, the state capitol. Kids with mikes started stirring up the crowd. SDS guys yelled "instructions:" "Now, here is what we gotta do. This thing won't be any good if you just let it last through today. We haven't made our points yet on this big march." Everyone yelled and screamed their assent. Fists were raised.

"We're going to form a city, the super drop-out city of all time, right here in Denver. It'll be a community of freaks where any freak in the world can come and live and work and play if he wants to. From there, we'll make our demands. Demands to stop this war, stop the draft, stop. . ."

The next day, a shanty town of tents and lean-to structures was erected on the Commons of the Denver University campus. Stolen wood, bricks, pieces of plastic, any kind of rubbish available was gathered to build the town. Kids dug into the ground, made campfires, had a lot of hard music, and spent a lot of time throwing frisbies.

The representatives presented their arguments to the university and sat back and waited. By now, there were over 2,000 people on five acres of ground, with poor sanitary conditions, little food, and no cooking utensils.

The people of Denver and the university administration were freaked out, but they wouldn't give in, and the students just stayed there playing with frisbies and yo yo's and kept waiting.

But the governor and the administration got together. They called the cops who moved in and razed the place. Within 24 hours, drop-out city was gone.

Within another 24 hours, 1,000 people had rebuilt it! This group was more determined — hard-line, yippie "pacificists." Four days after the rebuilding of the town, the students demanded the resignation of the Chancellor, Maurice Mitchell.

The faculty compromised on some of its demands, but Woodstock West, the name given the town, refused any compromise. Citizens were furious and demanded action.

IT'S GOOD TO KNOW

Meetings were held and the governor and administration declared, "Woodstock will go once and for all. Anyone still there will be arrested for trespassing." They planned a surprise move to demolish the town and arrest a bunch. . .

But the word got out. The students decided they'd have the last laugh. They would let the troops march in — to find nobody there.

Quietly, all night long, the population crept out. They holed up in the buildings on the University of Denver, in the library, around town . . . any place they could find.

At the peak hour of traffic in the morning through the oldest, most historic part of Denver, residents suddenly saw and heard the State! Police cars, Army jeeps, giant caterpillars, bulldozers, and excavation trucks rumbled and droned through quiet residential streets, interspersed with the boots of 1,000 National Guard troops marching up Evans Avenue to University Boulevard.

They were in full riot gear, armed and masked for tear gas. They were finally showing their colors! They were re-enacting right here in our own country what they'd been doing in Vietnam right along.

I laughed bitterly. My country!

I was justified in dropping acid, shooting speed, throwing bricks through windows. And more. Much, much more. . .

As the Guard moved in shoulder to shoulder and bumper to bumper, they found Woodstock West silent. They crashed and poked and kicked at anything in their way, hoping to find someone! They needed some scalps!

Three deep, they swept through the little shanty town, destroying it as they went, their bulldozers crawling over the flimsy shelters like something from *War of the Worlds.*

Finally, they came across one, solitary hippie, a guy who'd probably been so stoned he hadn't heard the noise of the previous night's evacuation. Even now, a trooper had to shake and poke him, and he was still so dazed that being yanked out of "bed" by a gas-masked armed Guardsmen didn't register. Finally, he did move — they gave him a swat on the jeans and sent him on his way.

Troopers loaded excavation trucks with debris. Other members of the Guard moved to the sidelines and looked on with the police and thousands of cheering bystanders.

By the end of the day, when those same people went back through the city on their way home from work, all they saw was five acres of torn up land, with big gaping holes and piles of wood and debris stacked up ready to be burned to the ground.

It had been good practice for both sides. I was elated, thinking of the Coming Attractions, and I determined to have a role in the next big scene.

8

OH I WANTED to fight. I wanted to help the SDS with the transfusion of man, and let blood like the old barbers did — let out the old, tired, sour blood that kept hearts from beating fast and free.

The only trouble was, the SDS used blackmail, too. Violence, fear, hate.

The rabble-rousers screamed and raved and jumped up and down and said all kinds of senseless things, like, "Now, I want you people to get it together and get out there and give them hell, man!"

One of the big leaders there was a typical rip-off type, getting others to do the dirty work and sitting back and watching the show. He was probably a sicko for arson, anyway. He used emotion to stir crowds up. They'd do anything that way.

But mine was a head trip. I thought there should be a rational approach, use logic, pursue intelligent programs. With that, then I could let go with the emotion and the blood-letting and the bombing and burning, overturning the pedestals on which the pig gods stood.

And, after that. . ?

I didn't know. It was too much. My head was spinning. Aching. Everything seemed fuzzy.

It was cold. Boulder was out of it. Winter in White was stalking me. I decided to split and warm up in the desert and try to get my head on straight, because if I was on a head trip, I had to use my head. Before I waded into the thick of the battle, I had to do some thinking.

I phoned a friend in Scottsdale, Rex Woodburn. "I'd like to come down and check out the scene," I said. "You got some room in your pad for me?"

"Sure, man. Make the trip, man."

"Ed?" I said after hanging up on Rex and going into the kitchen where he was dropping milk and crackers. "You want to cut some class time and accompany me down to Arizona?"

He did.

It was already snowing in the higher plateaus and mountainous country we drove through in our exodus from Colorado that October, but it was a golden transmutation once we dipped down out of those ice hills onto the Arizona desert in the full flush of Fall, then farther down onto the lower desert around Phoenix, where Summer never ends.

Rex lived near the high school in Scottsdale where my brother, Verne, had graduated. I'd met Rex through Verne.

Verne was there, and I was uneasy because he reminded me of myself. I was 19, Verne, 22, and neither of us were anywhere. And it was so illogical, coming from hardworking parents who had built a life for themselves . . . they were somewhere.

If either of us died tomorrow, no one would miss us. We were insignificant.

He also made me restless and bitter about not being able to go to school. Having Verne around to remind me of the nothingness of my life made me think of how I could lay tracks. Maybe if I gathered some money together to get to New York City. . .

But my resolution was weak. People around me had introduced me to some little flat green-brown buttons —

peyote. Each person has his own limit... you keep taking it until you can't take anymore. It's the worst tasting thing you can take, like drinking pure gasoline. The first button makes you want to get sick and die; by the second, you no longer feel pain; by the third, you're away in never-never land. On Number Four, you're a big man — in your own world, if you are anything at all.

Peyote is cactus — mescaline. The buds feel light, like cork. The Indians from a nearby reservation sold it to us. They would come up to the house with a grocery bag for which we paid from 7 to 16 cents per button "in bulk."

I could take four and be up, up, and away. Some of the Indians could take as many as 14 at a time. I don't know how long they stayed gone! Peyote played an important part in their religious ceremonies.

It was bad in a lot of ways, but it cured me of LSD. Acid is fluid, and like electronics. That's how it led to acid rock. Peyote was physically and psychically calm, "soft." It didn't bother me, inflame me like acid. It made me want to go out and lie under the stars and meditate.

LSD was one extreme, provoking irrational acts and violence. Peyote, on the other hand, gnawed away at my drive and resolution. I only worked because I had to. I worked at the Safari Hotel as a wine steward until about 3 a.m., then grabbed a girl and went home and slept until 8 a.m. Then we'd go out into the desert and lie in the sun naked, or wander along the river, serenely lost and alone, unworried, aimless, purposeless.

I decided I needed another change of scene. Scottsdale was falling apart. One of the guys we hung around with on "marijuana ranch" suddenly left. He decided to live in the mountains with the Indians and become a man of interior knowledge! The girls that Verne and another guy had brought with them also split. They were returning to a treehouse in Vermont.

And the locals were hard on me. Several times Arizona

cowboys — service station jocks, dishwashers, ditch diggers, bankers, whatever they might be, who were conscious of living in Arizona — would harrass me. Several of them beat me up and acted like I was an intruder, an outcast . . . guys who didn't even know me.

Did I have bad vibes? I was ready to split!

Near Jerome, doing about 80, the front wheel suddenly came off my VW, and I crashed into the side of the road. I was messed up, with a cut head and blood all over. I hadn't shaven for several days and I was a real gory specimen. I only had a few dollars on me, and I needed a pad to get cleaned up in and sack out until I felt better.

I finally managed to hail a cab driver and he took me to a motel. But they didn't like my looks. We tried another motel, then another and another. Nobody would give me a room. The cabbie finally took me to a fancy downtown hotel, went in, explained the situation, and they said okay.

After I got cleaned up, I phoned my dad and told him what happened.

"Well, get the car fixed," he answered. "I'll pay for it. I'll take care of your room, too."

In a couple of days, I was feeling better. My red VW was feeling better, too — after more than $100 worth of repairs. Deep inside me, a small voice said — "Your dad's a great guy. You can depend on him."

I kissed Arizona goodbye, but for some strange reason, the bad vibes seemed to come with me. The move didn't make me feel any different. It was like being a convict in the yard trying to get out of the spotlight, while all the time the tommy guns are blasting at him and every time he moves, the spotlight moves with him.

More appropriately, it was like trying to climb out of a deep hole and everytime you take a step upward, the hole moves upward with you. You carry the hole with you.

IT'S GOOD TO KNOW

It was the merry month of May, 1970, and the birds were high in the Pillar House.

The Pillar House was a cuckoo's nest of dope creeps in Boulder. An old house cut up into rooms, it was across the street from the University Townhouse Corporation houses. It was called Pillar House because one of its hyped-up hippie groupies had painted some psychedelic art on the pillars of the front porch — a good advertisement, because it was a pushing center, where you could always find someone to sell you dope. There were thousands of dollars worth of dope there most of the time.

Verne made that scene, too. I introduced him to the people I knew there, and we got together several times to jam with our guitars, sitars, and whatever.

One day, I was there with Kathy, the girl I'd known in high school, negotiating the sale of some dope toward my plane ticket to New York. We were standing on the porch rapping with a guy named David, when four frat types in a Mustang, whom I noticed had been circling the block a couple of times, pulled up to the curb, parked and got out.

I looked at Kathy and said, "This is a bust."

"You think so?" David asked.

"Yeah, yeah," I answered hastily. "I know the guys. They're pigs. Split!"

But they met us as we hurried down the steps. One of the guys stood in front of Kathy. "Do you live here?"

"No," she muttered. I shook my head and kept going.

Behind us, I heard them ask David and heard him answer yes. I heard the click of handcuffs.

At the same moment, three police cars pulled up, and cops stormed out carrying axes and narco bust kits. From the sidewalk, Kathy and I could see them bashing in the door.

I crept back up alongside of the house and peeked in a window. The cops had already chained nine guys and girls and set them on the floor under the stairs in the front entrance, irons arm to arm.

I went back to the sidewalk, and Kathy stuttered, "Why don't we get lost?"

"We've got to wait for Jim," I whispered urgently. Jim was one of our friends. He'd gone after more dope in my VW.

Suddenly, I froze. Verne's ultra super deluxe jewel of a 12-string guitar was in Jim's room. And it had a lot of grass and some speed, and a spoon — in the guitar case. And his name and address was on the lid! Oh, wow!

While I was still in orbit about that, I heard the growl of my bug, and Jim spun into the driveway. I screamed, "Jim, it's a bust. They're busting the house. Back up, back up. Get out. The pigs are here!"

He backed out, bumping over the curb, and not bothering to stop long enough to let me and Kathy in, buzzed off down the street.

A cop came out of the house and started for a police car. He was carrying Verne's beautiful guitar and the load of grass. It would be bad enough as it was, dope concealed in the guitar case, but Verne was on probation.

Kathy and I stood there on the sidewalk with other spectators, and in a few minutes, the rest of the cops came out. They had more evidence in hand — nine kids and an assortment of tangibles. People in the townhouses across the street were on their balconies raging against the bust, throwing tomatoes, bottles, full cans of beer, and yelling, "Don't touch those guys, you filthy pigs!"

More police arrived to quell that disturbance while police cars and a paddy wagon loaded up the flower people.

Kathy and I started looking for Jim and my little red VW. We started walking. Up one street, down another. Through alleys and backyards. I was really cussing Jim out. After two hours, we decided to take a short-cut through a park two blocks away from the Pillar House, a park we'd passed three times in our search. "What's that?" Kathy said, pointing into some trees.

IT'S GOOD TO KNOW 63

There was a spot of red shining through the leaves. It was the bug. Jim was gone. I never saw him again.

When Verne found out about the bust, he almost went out of his mind. He'd broken probation by going to Arizona, and now that he was safely back in Colorado, with the cops none the wiser, they'd found his guitar case with the marijuana in it, and he knew he'd get the death penalty, plus whatever else they could throw in. I put him on a bus for Steamboat Springs. "If anyone asks about you," I assured him, "I'll just say you're still in the State, but are working up in the mountains and they won't find you for centuries."

"What about my $1,000 guitar? It earned me a living, took me on two USO tours."

"Listen, Verne," I said, "I'll tell you what I'll do. I'll go in disguise to the hearing and see what's happening. I'll let you know."

The Greyhound took off, and in a few days, in my best theatrical makeup, I strode into the courtroom and turned up my hearing aid.

Some of the guys I knew took turns coming up before the judge as their names were called. Some of the names weren't responded to because the guys hadn't been caught in the net. When they came to Verne's name and read the warrant, I nearly cracked up.

The cops had recorded Verne's name incorrectly from the guitar case. They had him listed as Bernbullock. Anyone checking the name against a list of people on probation would be looking in vain under the b's for "Bernbullock."

I rushed to a phone to give him the good news.

At Steamboat Springs, Verne's off-again-on-again girlfriend, Val, said, "Verne's off again."

I went back to stay a few days in Littleton, and the very next day I got a phone call from Verne. He was calling from Santa Cruz, California.

Oh, God, no! I thought. He's really done it now. He's broken probation again and he was in the clear all along.

He sounded as down as down could be and my news didn't do anything to cheer him up. The only thing that would cheer him up even a little would be some bread, whatever I could send him. "Well, I have $18," I said. "I can send you that minus whatever it costs me to wire it."

"If you wouldn't mind," Verne murmured. He sounded so pathetic, what else could I do? Nothing, but send the money. And cry. I really did cry. The whole thing dramatized to what lows we'd sunk, both of us. Even my dope deal had been nipped in the bud by the untimely arrival of the cops, and if I was to get to New York City to make a fresh start, the only way I'd be able to do it now would be to sell my motorcycle.

But I knew I had to make a drastic change. Go somewhere completely different, foreign, new.

Ed said he'd go with me.

A week after I'd sent the money to Verne in California, I got another collect call from Verne. From Colorado Springs. "You playing hopscotch?" I asked.

"Something's happened," he said, and from the sound of his voice, it sounded like something really had. And knowing Verne, I knew it couldn't be anything good.

"Can you come and get me?" he asked, and I said sure and hung up. I called Ed, and the two of us went to Colorado Springs.

When we picked Verne up, he had a stranger with him, Devon Hartman, and a guitar — a sad imitation of the instrument the cops were holding, a squeaky and tinny learning guitar he'd picked up in a pawn shop for $2.50.

But something *had* happened to Verne — something so incredible that it really flipped Ed and me out of our minds. Verne started from the beginning. After picking up the money order and cashing it in Monterey, he'd started hitchhiking, bound for Southern California. Why? He didn't know. A van stopped — a van full of hippies. He got in. Where you heading? L.A.? Okay. It didn't really matter. The

IT'S GOOD TO KNOW

van stopped a couple more times to pick up more strays. No one knew where they were going. Just L.A.

At one of the stops, a long-haired guy got into the van and sat next to Verne. Just another freak. Someone lit up a joint, and they sang as they rolled down the highway, passing the joint from bum to bum. Verne was feeling bluer than blue, running from the law, afflicted with all kinds of wild urges, nothing but $15 in his levis, no fine guitar, and a probation violator. He took the joint, looked at it, sucked on it, passed it to the guy who had just gotten in.

"No, thanks," he said smiling. "I'm a Christian."

That was all. Verne felt as if the power of God had fallen, along with all the stars. He'd never known a hippie to turn down a joint, never had heard more profundity in five words — "No, thanks. I'm a Christian."

The guy didn't condemn him, didn't convict him. Just said five words.

Verne dropped the joint in the bottom of the van and, voice trembling, said, "I want to know what that means."

"My name's Eddie Weyman. I belong to what they call the Salt Company, run by Don Williams. It's a bunch of young Jesus People," Eddie chuckled. "They call us Jesus freaks. Praise the Lord, we are. We're freaked out on Jesus."

When they arrived in Los Angeles, Eddie said, "You still want to know what I mean?"

Verne nodded.

They went to the Virgil House on Virgil Street, and Verne met Don Williams and Devon Hartman, who was from Wichita, Kansas.

After telling us this much, Verne started strumming on the tinny guitar. For some reason, the music sounded pretty good. I couldn't believe my ears. Then I *really* couldn't believe my ears when Ed asked, "Then what?" and Verne said, "I got Jesus."

"You got to be kidding!"

"No. Jesus saved me. He can save you."

I was completely stunned. When Verne looked at me, my mouth worked, but I couldn't say anything.

Ed spoke for me. "Hey, Verne, it's just another of your freaked out illusions, right? What've you been on this time? Something we don't know about?"

"Just Jesus," Verne said.

"Shut up!" Ed shouted. He seemed to be afraid. "If you want to talk about something, talk about something constructive and not about Jesus Christ."

I finally found my voice and said, "Yeah, man. There's a whole life to be lived and a war to fight and some cities to tear down and some trips to take. And you freak out on a Jesus kick. You must be out of your head."

When we arrived home, Verne went immediately to the district attorney and told him he'd violated his probation and had even had grass in his guitar case. Also that he'd gone to California and found Jesus and wanted to go back there and live with some Christians. I expected him to be escorted to the maximum security block or to the psychiatric ward of General Hospital.

I freaked out of my mind when Verne came back home with some official looking papers in his hands and announced, "He said I could go to California and they are dropping all the charges."

I wondered if I was hearing right, if maybe I wasn't starting to crack up myself. It was too much. Then I figured what he was up to. He'd deliberately put on the corny Christian act just to get the cops to let him go. My big brother, the dummy who was always sticking both feet in his mouth and swallowing them clear to his gut, finally got wise after all. Finally learned about cool. He had one-upped the pigs and used Jesus and got away with it. I smiled.

But now I knew that Ed and I had to split right away. Too much of this wasn't good for our constitutions. We'd go to New York City, and I'd enroll in the School of Dramatic Arts,

IT'S GOOD TO KNOW

and when I wasn't in a play, we'd be politically active and tearing up the sidewalks of New York. We were going to hit that city hard.

None of this Jesus stuff for us. We'd knock the Jesus out of the fat piggy Establishment and set up free love, free living, and free dope. I didn't need God. He'd be needing me!

I drove to the airport early the next morning, and I had just enough time to phone my father.

"Airport?" Dad asked, flabbergasted. "You going somewhere, again?"

"Just to New York," I said. "I knew you and Mom were busy, and I'm always so much trouble, Ed and I just took care of ourselves."

"You should've told me —"

"You've been great, Dad. If we bothered you every time we were on a bummer, you wouldn't get anything done. Nothing at all. You're too much, Dad. . ."

I had to hang up. The plane was about ready to close its door. . .

And I was crying.

9

I'D GONE TO New York for a new start, to find myself. But first I had to find people, the kind of people who fed my ego and made me feel as though I was somebody, people who were in some way radical, non-Establishment. And I had to orient myself to the all-important dope set-up. I didn't realize it, but I was drifting into the same old patterns.

It wasn't until Fall that I met someone who turned out to be superactive in political agitation. I answered an ad which read, "graduate student requires assistance in production of film."

The student turned out to be a strange guy in his thirties with an Omar Sharif look. Known as Quicksilver, he dressed in Army khakis and affected a military stance which complimented his moustache and chronically stiff neck. A most peculiar guy.

Quicksilver was aptly named. He was studying movie production at the New School for Social Research, near New York University, and his mind seemed to be going at a million frames a minute. He was the center of hustle and bustle and preoccupied with everything revolving around him. When I finally got his attention and indicated my interest in the ad, he had to think a minute, then said, "We need a man for an alley scene. You look like you might fit. We're doing a *cinema verite* thing. We take the camera outside and shoot actual happenings which suggest a story line to us. Later, we'll firm it up with a lot of editing. Gives the effect of stark realism."

I glanced around at several girls assembled in the classroom where our interview had taken place. Realism? They wore old, antique clothing — old shawls, long dresses from the 1890's, peasant costumes. The gals looked dangerous with their long, spiky fingernails in weird colors to match their lipstick. I shuddered, remembering the asylum scene in *Marat/Sade*.

Even more mysterious, during my visits I'd overhear little hush-hush conversations, catch words and phrases such as, "On May Day . . . medical units for the injured . . . blockade the Capitol."

Eventually they shot me wandering out of an alley carrying a box. I popped up several times during the movie, without speaking any lines, and my part in the whole film was as mysterious as the other business I kept overhearing.

I finally forced Quicksilver to give me a couple of minutes of his valuable time. "What's this about storming the Capitol?" I asked.

I could tell he still regarded me with suspicion.

"Listen," I said, "I'm interested. I'm sick of the war and the fat pigs."

Before he'd tell me anything, he threw a lot of questions at me about myself and what I had been into. Finally he seemed satisfied and outlined the basics. Protesters were to cut off Washington, DC, from all supply routes and starve the politicians into submitting to a list of demands. There was going to be a lot of excitement. That turned me on!

I had to come back a couple of times to get the full picture, and it convinced me that the film thing was literally theater of the absurd. Quicksilver was concerned with routing mass numbers of protesters, and I suggested I could help out by driving a bus, if transportation was one of their hang-ups. He didn't seem too interested in that. I then volunteered to draw up a riot manual to advise protestors on how to groove in on the action without too much hassle.

I'd actually drawn up some instructions for other groups, somewhat like a military field manual. That he dug, and even pointed out I would need to visit Washington to get some background. And they were dead earnest: the riot was being planned more than six months in advance and would involve up to 200,000 people.

I was working at two different jobs, and Ed and I were studying drama at Herbert Berghof's Drama School. We'd finally solved the accommodation problem, after playing musical pads for the first few weeks in the city. The first room Ed and I checked into when we arrived in New York was in a well-known international chain of "hotels," catering to men only, and the particular "link" we stayed at — for one night — contained the largest collection of missing links I'd ever seen.

We soon discovered that Greenwich Village was loaded with homosexuals. An especially odd couple lived a few flights up from the apartment we found, a glorified hotel room renting for a cool $250 a month. Ed was later lured from the apartment to a real tender trap. A fellow student in the drama school had a nice, well-furnished pad, which included a Steinway piano. He said he'd welcome Ed to share the place with him in exchange for helping with the rent. It was such a good deal and Ed couldn't resist it. He didn't consider that strings other than piano strings might be attached. In two weeks he confessed sheepishly that his new roommate had turned out to be "one of those," and wouldn't give him a minute's peace.

But I'd been left holding the bag for the steep rent on the Greenwich Village cubbyhole, and by the time Ed saw the handwriting on the wall and wanted to move back in with

IT'S GOOD TO KNOW

me, I had already given up the place. Ed decided he had had it with New York and flew back to Colorado.

In the meantime, I had gotten a part-time job as a waiter, and filled in the rest of the work day as a supervisor for Cosmic Messengers.

I found out about the messenger service when I answered an ad in Greenwich Village's famous, *Village Voice* newspaper: "WANTED, MOTORCYCLE MAINTENANCE SUPERVISOR." I appeared at the address, and the owner, Harry Ferguson, a guy who looked like a surfer, asked if I had any tools.

I replied, "Yes, if you can call them that." My best were still in Colorado, but I would send for them.

As it worked out, my job schedule, including the restaurant job was quite hectic: I'd get up bright and early in the morning, zip out to the Cosmic Messenger garage and make sure the bikes had gasoline and were in running order. I'd check out the various drivers or messengers waiting in the dispatch office for an assignment, which could be the delivery of a parcel or document anywhere in the greater New York area. Then I would take the subway uptown to the Roast Beef and Brew Restaurant where I was a lunch waiter. I would return in the afternoon to see that all the bikes were checked in and maintained. On certain evenings, I went to Herbert Berhof's Drama School.

As an employee of Cosmic Messengers, it was not long before I found myself pinch-hitting on the driving part when there was an unexpected volume of business or someone was knocked out. It was an experience that taught me more about the geography and social conditions of New York than most natives could get in a lifetime. Buzzing from one end of town to the other, delivering stuff from City Hall to the City Zoo, I met all kinds of people and animals in a very short time.

Even the beginning of the day was interesting, just waiting for a call. One by one, the six to eight messengers would show up at the dispatch office, a little store-front hole in the wall in a funky old building in Greenwich Village. We sat around waiting for a run, jawing, drinking coffee, and sometimes blowing a joint. There was usually poker being played as we waited for our girl, Sissy, to alert us. For awhile we got in the habit of drinking tequila with our poker, taking a double shot with lemon and salt and slugging it down.

I soon discovered that almost every business in New York City had a "resident gangster" who took a cut for "protection." We often had a couple of visitors — New York gangsters who had some kind of connection with the organization and used their influence with captive cops to fix traffic tickets when our drivers were overly zealous.

Our customers included the major broadcasting companies, newspapers, government officials, even the Mayor. Several times His Worship needed to get something signed properly by someone uptown. He'd buzz Cosmic.

We kept track of our deliveries by having sender and receiver sign forms. There was a $3.50 fee for the first zone, another $2 for each zone thereafter. More bread for a super-rush, special handling, too big, too small. We had a van for larger deliveries.

Even counting the extra pay for working as messenger along with my steady pay as the maintenance supervisor for Cosmic and my pay and tips as a waiter for the Roast Beef and Brew, New York City's toll on my wad was still a real grab, and I quickly grabbed at other opportunities to add to the wad as fast as it was peeled away. I resumed my former "pharmaceutical" merchandising practice by delivering a little grass to a following I developed from scratch. Some of these customers were Madison Avenue ad agencies. I left no turn unstoned to beef up my bread.

I was developing a kind of empire. As a bike enthusiast from way back, I had to include my driving as one of the fringe benefits I enjoyed as I got to know the whirl of the fantastic city. New York to a Cosmic Messenger turned out to be a motorcyclist's dream. You could drive at high speed,

IT'S GOOD TO KNOW 73

weaving in and out of traffic, bugging the cops, as you shot on by twenty miles an hour faster than they could get out of their little Vespas.

New York driving was totally insane. Insane driving, dizzy drivers, crazy cabbies. You could be off your rocker, retarded, or gay, you could have any neurosis or psychosis in the book, any kind of problem, and you could always feed your sickness in New York. If no other city in the world will take you, New York, the realm of the world misfits, will.

I was always rocked by the fact that you could walk on the same street at the same time, day in and day out, and never see the same human being twice. Such a mass of humanity was crashing along, I loved it, yet, I hated it. It was the worst place in the world and the best.

I was beginning to make enough money to enjoy life again, and I wondered why I'd felt so low a few months back. As I started to recall those times it wasn't too hard to see why. After Ed had split it wasn't easy coming up with $250 a month. I was behind to begin with; I hadn't even paid the security deposit. I owed something like $500, and in that area they got a little physically tough when they came collecting.

They did come a few days later. A couple of the landlord's boys came around, and when I repeated the same stupid lies for about the fourth time, one grabbed me while the other gave me a kick. "That's how we're going to kick you out in the street, buddy," he growled. "You'd better have the dough by the time we walk up those stairs again."

With my last few bucks, I went to the White Horse Tavern to think about what I could do — and get drunk. New York was full of bars. Bars take on a kind of personality and reflect the neighborhood. Whatever your gig was in New York City, you could find your place. I liked the "horses" at the White Horse Tavern. The patrons ran the gamut from the formally dressed and ultra-wealthy to artists and musicians.

Sometimes I played chess in the back room while drinking

Kaluha cut with milk, over ice, a slow, easy drink to go on all night, which might mean until 4 a.m.

That night I wasn't interested in chess or coffee drinks. I just wanted a bite to eat and booze. "Lay me on a gut bomb and scotch," I told Janice, the barmaid. A gut bomb was a hamburger.

I had become acquainted with this strange barfly from previous visits. In her spare time she did illustrating. She had a mania for criminals and had done a lot of pen-and-ink treatments of Charlie Manson.

Janice ran around with a couple of hoods who, despite the fact that they weren't very welcome there, would come into the White Horse and boast about the neat ways they'd evaded being caught for one robbery or the other.

Janice was 28, 5 feet, 10 inches tall and somewhat heavy at 150 pounds. She had no father while growing up in the Virgin Islands and her mother had kicked her around. She was drunk half the time and extremely moody. The only place I'd seen her really happy was while she was slinging drinks at the White Horse.

That night Janice gave me another glass of scotch, then said, "What's eating you?"

I told her what had happened, then added, "I'll be out in the street any day now. How do you like them apples?"

Janice shrugged. "I hate them." She swallowed a lump in her throat.

I stared at her. I always knew she was emotional. I hadn't realized she liked me enough to go clucky over my misfortune. Now her eyes were moist.

"Listen, hon," she finally said. "You know something about me. I mean, you know the kind of crowd I dig. Bobby, Johnny Machine. . .

"What about it?"

"First . . . do you like cats?"

I nodded.

"How about dogs?"

IT'S GOOD TO KNOW

"Arf, arf."

"Well, you know I have a big apartment on the Lower East Side. I've got an extra bedroom. The boys never stay there overnight when they come around. They're always at some swanky hotel suite or they're on the lam. My place would be the first place the cops would come if Bobby or Johnny got busted."

"Yeah, yeah. Well. . ?"

"You could — move in."

I took a deep breath. There had to be a catch. Hesitantly, expecting the worst, I said, "What's the tab?"

"Well, I pay $95 a month, Rand. I'd charge you $50."

"Wait. How come you only pay $95 when I have to pay a cool $250 for the elevated gopher hole I've been living in?"

"Everyone in the world has heard of Greenwich Village. Artists, writers, anyone like that . . . they think they'll become famous if they claim a Greenwich Village address. But who the hell has ever bragged about living on the Lower East Side?"

"Yeah, yeah. Well, how soon can I move?"

"Tonight."

The Lower East Side is the worst place in the world to live. One would be safer in the jungle with vipers. On Janice's block alone there were 4,000 people, men, women, children. Men trying to raise their families in the midst of crime, dirt, ugliness, a place where life means no more to anybody than a rat in the street. Dark, dingy, ugly. Janice's apartment was just on the borderline. Mostly Puerto Ricans lived on her side of the street, with a sprinkling of Chinese. But across the street were heroin junkies and prostitutes. Just crossing the street put you into Hell.

Janice's apartment was on the fourth floor. You could scale the 12 flights of stairs up to it and have time for a coffee break before the elevator made it. But it had one of New York's rare commodities: space! There was the extra bedroom, a kind of library, a dining room, and, at the end of a long hall, the living room and a kitchen.

When I got back to my apartment in the early hours, I got everything together and then went upstairs and woke up one of the two gays living above me. "I've got something to sell you if you two plan on raising a family," I said. "A real classy Oriental rug. Worth $500 but I'll let it go for $100."

"Okay, we'll give you $75, Randy," Alphie said, rubbing his eyes. "Gino will like it. He's still asleep. I was just wondering what I could give him for a birthday present." He hesitated. "But . . . can I have it on a $20 down and pay the rest next week?"

I grunted and shrugged. "All right . . . where's the $20?"

He already had it out of his wallet.

"You have to get it out tonight, before the landlord knows what you're up to," I said. "And thanks."

I was busy from a little after six in the morning until late at night, and Janice worked most nights, so I didn't see much of my new roommate. She didn't seem to be much interested in sex with me, and quite a few times when I'd come in someone was in her bedroom with her. Sometimes I came in for a short stop on my way across town, and I'd find Bobby Gillespie in the living room talking with her. A few times Johnny Machine was with him.

These two guys could just look at you and ice would form on your head. I'd already become acquainted with several gangsters a' la New York; it seemed as though every business I heard about was forced to tie up with some hood or other. But some of these Mafia type gangsters I'd met or heard about seemed like kittens compared with Bobby and Johnny. They were mean from the word go, and if they were there, I just excused myself and went to my room. And locked the door.

To look at him, you might not have guessed that Bobby was a killer type; he had a slight build and light, sandy colored hair. Around thirty years old, he was very quiet and

IT'S GOOD TO KNOW

introspective. If you looked at his hard, steel blue eyes, you knew. Good-looking, dark-eyes Johnny Machine gave himself away with his loud, vulgar mouth. He was brash and pushy.

I couldn't help overhearing things, and during a period when they were almost constantly in the apartment, huddling with Janice and with Johnny Machine's girlfriend, Greta, I gradually pieced together that they were planning a wild cross-country crime spree. They had their guns on the table, detective revolvers with short barrels. On the day they evidently were to take off, I came home to pick up some tools and found Janice's bags near the door. She was standing unsteadily beside them. She handed me a set of keys. "I'm waiting for Bobby to pick me up," she hiccoughed. "I'm druuuunk as a lady."

"Hmmmmm. Going on a holiday?"

"A working holiday," she giggled. "I may be gone for quite some time, so don't hold my room open for me necessarily. You can take over the lease . . . see, I signed it over to you. I knew you wouldn't mind."

I shrugged. She could very well be gone permanently. No telling where she might end up: in Mexico, Paris, the bottom of the Atlantic Ocean with her feet in a bucket of cement.

So I had the pad all to myself. And with the extra bread beginning to come in, life was really taking on a shine.

I preferred our "tame," resident gangsters, John Clarke and Joe LeProtto, who had a little office near Cosmic Messengers but spent a great deal of their time "supervising" the supervisors at Cosmic. They evidently had a cut in with Harry Ferguson, who had built up the Messengers. John and Joe were the kind of crooks you could reason with. You did what they told you, but you could reason with them. What was the difference whether they shook people down?

They always did it with a smile, a joke . . . unless someone got unreasonable with them.

Brian Hurst, an Englishman who'd come to work for Cosmic, got away with murder with these two guys. He was the one who coined the term, "resident gangsters," and when he called them that to their face, they pretended to hit the ceiling. But they liked jokes, too.

Once Brian said, "Tell me, John, old chap, what's it like being a gangster, anyway?"

"Why, you --- I'm going to take Sam to you if you call me names."

"Sam? Who's Sam?" Brian asked, feigning innocence.

John pulled out his gun, a shiny nickelplated Smith & Wesson .38. "This is Sam." He held it right up to Brian's head. "Sam, are you going to talk? Listen, jerk, Sam's going to talk to you if you don't watch your mouth."

"Hmmmm," Brian said. "That's intriguing. Do most gangsters carry guns?"

They dug Brian, but I'd heard of a few other people who'd had holes dug for them because of these funny gangsters. Sam was for real, man.

They were also good for arm-twisting if we needed something right away. They worked in pairs, a muscle man and a brains man, Joe being the sharpie and carrying all the money, John, the gun. Joe was about 5'9", slight of build, wore wire-rimmed rose-tinted glasses, dark hair and was very, very, Italian. When he was being a sharpie his dark eyes and pointed lower lips didn't show off his big smile. As soon as he had made his point a fast easy grin would appear again.

Joe had been raised in Little Italy and he had apartments all over town. He had other interests beside the Cosmic Messengers, and I suspected he was a pretty big guy in Little Italy.

But crime wasn't my bag. The only real friend I had while I was working for Cosmic Messengers was Lucky, who

IT'S GOOD TO KNOW

worked there, too. We became friends the first night I met him, and I offered to share my pad with him, when the time came he needed one. He'd been in Denver, where he'd had a girlfriend. We were sure we had seen each other there hanging around hippie bars. He was 28, over six-feet tall, like me, and like me, thin. He had a moustache and goatee the same color as his dishwater brown hair, which was thick and fairly long. A parachute tatooed on his arm was a memento of paratrooper days in Vietnam. He was a quiet, humble guy, with a catchy laugh and big, broad smile. Lucky was lots of fun, and we kidded each other. He called me "Dr. Bullock," and I called him "Sergeant."

We perfected a system for driving uptown on his 100cc Honda. He'd sit in front, and I'd reach from behind him to handle the controls. We did that flat out as fast as we could drive going up 7th Street to get to O'Leary's Irish bar uptown.

When I told Lucky about what was going on with Quicksilver, the big plans being drawn up to bring Uncle Sam to his knees so he'd listen to reason about the war and the draft, Lucky's eyes lit up. He had been in Vietnam and had first-hand experience with the scene. He wanted in.

While the filmmaking with Quicksilver was going on and the other plan was brewing, I was really studying drama under Herbert Berghof. Herbert and his wife, Uta Hagen, were both famous around Broadway. Herbert had been a drama coach for Marlon Brando. We did a lot of scene work, performing short scenes and being critiqued by eight to 16 people.

My association with the Berghof organization led to one good and one bad relationship in my life. First, the good. I walked into the White Horse Tavern one night and a black guy named Bruce McKeethen, who spoke with an educated Eastern dialect, came up to me and told me he had an appointment to do a scene in front of all the casting directors at NBC. It had taken him nine months to get in. He needed a scene partner for the screen test coming up soon.

"I saw you working out at Berghof's," Bruce said. "You have a great style. Would you do this with me?"

"Sure," I said, after picking myself up off the floor.

"We have some time to work on it. Why don't you come over to my apartment?"

I nodded. Already, we somehow knew we both smoked grass.

We went to his apartment. And smoked grass. Then Bruce said, "I have to go out for a few minutes."

While he was gone, there was a knock on the door. It was a girl I'd seen before at the White Horse, Susan Tyes. We stood on either side of the doorway and stared blue into blue. Something sparked between us.

When Bruce came back I suggested we all go over to the Cookie Bar, where the theater crowd hung out, and have a gut bomb. We did just that. But Bruce seemed rather uptight.

When I saw him alone, he said, "Randy, Susan's bad news. Keep away from her."

"Well, hell, Bruce," I said, annoyed. "What's the problem? I mean, I can tell we really like each other." I paused and looked at him. "You and she aren't serious about each other, are you? I mean, if you are, okay. That's great. But you didn't act like it."

Bruce shook his head and stared at the floor. "She's, like — evil. She'll sap you, take you for all you're worth. Randy, you can really make it, the way you're going. *If* you keep away from Susan."

I shrugged. "I can handle chicks —"

Bruce gave a bitter laugh. "She'll hurt you, man. She'll end up hurting you hard."

During the next few weeks when I found opportunities to see Susan, I looked for any telltale signs that what Bruce said might be true. But she looked just fine to me. And she made love like it was going out of style. To me, sex was the supreme test, and she passed it with flying colors. I sometimes even entertained the idea I was falling in love with her . . . me, the guy who had given up on love.

But every time Susan and I were with Bruce, Bruce was jittery. I kept asking myself why? And why should he care what happened to me anyway? I was sure the real reason was because he had a grudge against Susan. He probably had had an affair with her that turned sour.

Bruce and I were still looking for the right scene to do together, and I didn't want to lose this chance. The difficulty, besides Susan, was finding a good scene for a white and a black man. Suddenly, I had a brainstorm. I called Bruce and said, "I have the scene to do."

When we got to NBC, I was wearing little wire glasses and a moustache. They wanted to know what the name of the play was. I said, *"Love, Susan,* by Ed Kane. It's not published, yet."

We proceeded to do an impromptu skit about a girl we both knew, who really was Susan Tyes. For the conflict, we simply repeated one of our typical arguments about Susan.

The casting director said, "Well, Mr. Bullock there are some things we could use you for in the future." They accepted some of my publicity photos and told me they'd let me know.

When I phoned Bruce up a couple of days later, he said, "Oh, yeah, man, I went to work for them the next day. I got $80 for a walk-on part. And they've got me lined up for a lot of soap-opera work on TV. Fabulous bread. Thanks for helping."

"Yeah. And, you, thanks," I hung up.

I didn't get any work out of that episode, but I did get Susan Tyes — 5 feet 5, with curly, flippy blond hair and sad blue eyes . . . sad, I found out, because of her father dying. It had happened two years ago, but it still bugged her. She had a young hippie brother, Joe, who lived in a shack with a girl in Cape Cod. And she had a dog named Brandy who had a complex.

Susan was 23 years old. She was a pretty good actress after all, I began to see. She acted the part of the dumb blond, but she was dumb like a fox. She didn't do anything against me though, and I couldn't see where Bruce had gotten all his anxieties about her. Of course, I sometimes wondered why Brandy was so neurotic. . .

10

BY THE TIME February rolled around, the fuel strike that had practically paralyzed New York, had come to a halt. We had hot water in the pipes again, we were warm again. I had used Susan Tyes during the fuel strike, used her pad — and her — to keep warm. And now it was her turn, as I slowly discovered.

"Randy," she cooed on my shoulder one night, "can I move in with you? I'm about to be kicked out of here. I owe three months' rent, and I've already lost my security deposit."

"Of course, baby," I drawled, my arm around her waist. "I don't even know how long I'll be here. I may want to go back to Colorado. We could have a co-interest in the apartment, and you could take over when I split."

When I told Lucky she was moving in with us, all he would say was, "I got a bad feeling about that chick, Dr. Bullock." And no amount of bullying would bring any amplification out of him. But he did come through with some muscles for moving.

Since Susan was so far behind in her rent, we decided that a move at 1 a.m. in the morning would be appropriate. Lucky and I got a truck, backed into a place that didn't look too conspicuous, and, piece by piece, we moved out her couch, two big chairs, and a whole raft of junk she just couldn't let go. Since we had to hurry, we weren't very careful, but Susan was sweet and loving right through the whole ordeal.

Then, one by one, piece by piece, we had to move the stuff up the stairs of our apartment building, 12 flights!

"I'm sorry about all this stuff, Randy," she cooed in my ear that morning as we fell into bed. "I'll get it straightened out this week . . . and I'll cook up some good meals for you and Lucky. You won't be sorry you took me in."

"Look, baby," I answered, "as long as you keep my bed this warm, I don't care what kind of stuff you bring around. Take your time getting settled in."

It took her about a week to unpack her clothes, and every closet in the place was bulging. Lucky didn't have much in his closet, so I begged a few feet of space from him.

Susan and I had some real groovy dope deals going, and between my two jobs, I was making over $400 a week. And spending it. We should have been flying high. I had just bought a new stereo and lots of records, a small TV and an FM receiver, and a wardrobe of new clothes. Some of this was an effort to please Susan, some just my own greed.

So I couldn't stop making money. Every time a deal came up to buy or sell dope, I grabbed at it. When Susan and I were talking business, she was all right. But after the first couple of weeks, the minute I told her I'd be out late for one reason or another, I'd get hit with a barrage of words. Dirty words. "Don't lie to me again, you -----, I know you're going to be with that girl in the drama group tonight, practicing your part in that stupid play."

One morning, I got up at the usual time, 6:30, ready to start another day by going with Lucky to the café where we could get 65¢ eggs, potatoes, bacon, and coffee that cost $2.50 everywhere else.

I was despondent. I just couldn't seem to get moving. I dressed and went out into the other room to wait for Lucky. But I was restless and moody. I went back into our bedroom and sat down on the floor by the bed. Susan woke up. "What are you doing?" she screamed.

I jumped. "Just sitting here. What does it look like? For God's sake, what's the big deal?"

"Get out of here. Get out!"

When I told Lucky about it on our way to Ruby's, he finally let loose with his opinion of Susan. I didn't even try to defend her. I didn't understand her any more than he did.

In a couple of weeks, Susan had become the meanest, nastiest person I had ever met. I couldn't even touch her without having my head bitten off.

Oh, the bread was rolling in, dope deals hanging fire, a groovy pad for only $95 a month. I had two jobs, both paying good money. The big Triumph bike was mine, worked off in six easy payments. There was money in the bank.

But Susan wasn't satisfied. She decided she wanted more company than I could give her. One night there was a knock on the door. It was Bob Wentworth, a guy Susan and I had met at the White Horse. I'd been impressed that he had been road manager of "The Crazy World of Arthur Brown," a rock and roll show.

"Uh, I called today," Bob said. "Susan said it would be all right if I came over and stayed for a while. I'm in need of a pad."

I shrugged. "Well, if she said that . . . well, help yourself to the couch. The other rooms are taken." I waved him over to the couch and told him where to put his things.

Susan was in the kitchen; now she came into the living room. She had been on a new kick of macrobiotics and I couldn't go for all the dried fruits that went with it, figs, dates, raisins, and more figs. In everything.

I said, "Uh, Bob. I hope you like figs, dates, raisins, and brown rice. It's a real food trip."

"Of course I do," Bob replied. "I'm the one who turned Susan onto all that."

I stared at him for a minute, then at Susan, and the light zinged on in my head. I slammed the door on my way out.

It was my night to report in to Quicksilver, and I was in a good mood for planning a riot. This would be my last night in New York, for a while anyway. Lucky and I were hopping a ride to D.C., to map out an escape route for yippies when they staged the big show.

The meeting was short and quick that night, and Lucky and I decided to head for D.C. early in the a.m. We went to the White Horse and drank beer. "You got all that info on who to contact when we get to Washington?" Lucky asked.

I pulled out my list. I hadn't had a chance to look at it until now. One name I recognized. "Get a load. He's with *Time* Magazine. A real biggy." I flipped through the rest of the list. There were names and places of people who'd put us up in D.C. One was in Georgetown . . . a big man.

Till now, we'd just been little cogs in the wheel.

In D.C., we phoned the guy in Georgetown. He gave us some names of other contacts. He was cordial and helpful, and urged us to contact him if there was any trouble.

We did the tour, noting churches and parks where yippies could stay. We sketched maps of these parks and of the major intersections of the downtown area near the White House and the Washington Monument. It was important that everyone have an escape route in mind, so they needed to know the inroads and outroads and what bridges would be blockaded. We even made drawings of girders of bridges that could be crawled along if you were being chased, and cased out sewers where yippies could hide.

I was feeling great! At last, I was in my element, doing what I'd come to the East Coast to do.

As we took notes and drew sketches we jotted down anything that came into our minds to help the demonstrators, like, "Don't take any ID with you. Put numbers of addresses and phone numbers of contacts on your arm. If you get busted, you won't have any ID papers." We did

IT'S GOOD TO KNOW 87

some research on the phone company and decided to include in our manual some phone numbers of people who would help yippies if they were in trouble. We included some credit card numbers that could be used to charge calls against, and directions for making "beeper boxes" that would confuse phone company computers.

We scoped out the East Mall area of the Potomac Park, site of the main meeting place, and we listed some university buildings that could provide temporary refuge. Most of the protesters would sack out in the park. Our *Time* magazine correspondent assured us all of this would get the right kind of publicity.

Just before we returned to New York we scouted out a few stores to see which ones would be easy to steal from, and a few restaurants easy to walk out of without paying.

When we reported to Quicksilver, I could tell by the way he kept pulling at his moustache that he really dug what we'd done.

Back with Susan, I tried to look at her more objectively. I decided to leave her alone for a while and see what she'd do about us. I got my answer soon. It was obvious that Bob and she were having an affair.

I just put more time into the manual. It was shaping up as a tabloid 15 inches long, with six pages crammed with all the general items Lucky and I had discovered. I pasted in funky underground art for offset, and the whole thing was foldable like *Rolling Stone* magazine.

My work put me "in." I was invited to Bobby Dylan's 30th birthday party, a huge block affair. He made a brief appearance and looked uptight. I was more intrigued with Abbie Hoffman, famous for his performance at the Fabulous Chi Seven Festival, otherwise known as the conspiracy trial of the Chicago Conspirators. And for his skill with the yo yo.

I walked up on his wrong side, and he was immediately suspicious of me. I guess we had bad vibes. I knew he was involved in May Day, as half the party guests were, but I didn't know how to clue him in that I was doing great things for the cause. So we just talked about yo yo's.

Dylan's party turned out to be the only social event I attended before May Day. I was interested in all these people, but I wasn't sure I fit in the way they did. They seemed weird. People with money and class were roaming around, celebrating some singer's birthday with dancing, drinking, smoking, and a lot of noise, yet the birthday boy wasn't even there!

I went home, cold and blue. I didn't know where Susan was. At some tavern with Bob, I guessed. While I got ready to take a shower and warm up, a song came on the radio I had heard before — "Put Your Hand in the Hand of the Man Who Stills the Water. . ."

"Put your hand in the hand of the Man who calms the sea./ Take a look at yourself, and you can look at others differently./ By putting your hand in the hand of the Man from Galilee."

A voice came on the radio, a low, deep voice. A guy was rapping about God and what he could do for me. Somehow I couldn't seem to reach over and turn it off. I stood there and listened to his whole spiel.

It got me to thinking about my folks. Dad and Mom had written occasionally, but I hardly ever answered. If something happened to me, they'd never know. Mom had sent a paper called *Speak Out,* which showed what Verne was doing in California. I read the stories about Verne. "This is my brother? Hah! They were just using him as a singer and trying to show him as a good example. I laughed out loud. I ought to write them a letter and tell them what he's really like; then they could see what their goody-goody hero is."

I piled into bed thinking about that letter. But why bother? I'd heard that Ed had also crashed. Ed, a Jesus Freak! Why did they have to go off the deep end? I dropped off finally, but not before taking a downer.

The next day was one of those cold, grey mornings that

IT'S GOOD TO KNOW

can only happen in New York. I was annoyed because Susan hadn't even bothered to make an appearance. When I checked into Cosmic, they had a lousy run lined up for me, and I had to use my own bike, as two of their machines were down. Worse, the destination was in Harlem, and I knew the traffic would be solid, cars crawling because there was ice in the streets, the kind of black patches you don't see until you're right on top of them.

I took off carefully, having almost broadsided someone on my way to the office. A guy needs a tank in weather like this, I thought. Some crud swished by me and threw slush up in my face and I had to stop to wipe it off. From then on, I kept to the center of the street and made the cars tag along behind me.

Another guy came up right behind me and laid on his horn.

"You dirty ---!" I yelled back at him, turning around to wave my gloved fist. I also gave him a signal, but it was too late. In turning around, I missed the sharp detour I was supposed to make around some construction and hit a bridge abutement, head on!

They had to bring the van clear from downtown to pick me up. My TR was bent out of shape but, aside from a few cuts and scratches and headache, I was okay.

I went home to bed and slept a while, then woke up to hear screaming and yelling and laughing out in the living room.

Lucky came in to check on me. "Dr. Bullock, you're going to be upset, but your charming little girlfriend just brought another stud home."

"Oh, great," I moaned. Just a few days ago, a couple of Janice's friends from the Virgin Islands, Marty and Penny, had popped up, not knowing Janice was God-knows-where, and asked if they could flop for a week. They were flopping in the other bedroom and Lucky was occupying the long hall while they were here. "Full house and jokers wild," I muttered.

Lucky put a hand on my shoulder. "Dr. Bullock, why don't you go out there and tell him to take off. And Susan too while you're at it?"

I was awake by now. Awake and aching. And mad.

Susan was on the couch with some jerk she had probably picked up on the street, a pimply faced rat of a kid. They'd just dropped some acid.

Susan looked up when I barged into the room, but instead of showing any guilt, she started raving at me about the apartment. "I wouldn't mind some privacy," she stormed. "I'm sick of being interrupted. I want this apartment, all to myself. You didn't keep your promise..."

Like a flash, it hit. That's what she'd been after all along. Not me. My apartment. Apartments were like investing in land. Between the two of us, we had about $3,000 worth of stuff in that pad. She didn't want much! Still, I had opened my big fat mouth and told her I'd probably split for Colorado some time.

"Listen, we'll discuss our private business after our little friend here is gone," I said. I yanked the guy off the couch and started shoving him across the room. He was screaming and crying at me to let him go, but I didn't stop until he was out of the door.

Susan followed him, stomping out into the hall and yelling.

I was almost deranged. I'd taken dope to ease the pain of the accident and hadn't had enough time to sleep it off. Lucky and Bob had come out to watch the fireworks and they'd cheered me on. Now that Susan and her creepy friend had gone, we relaxed on the floor and I reached over and turned on the stereo.

There was a knock on the door and we all jumped up, ready for more action if necessary. But it was a couple of girls we knew. We were glad to have some pleasant company.

Bob was restless. He got up and went to the back of the

place to take out the trash. I knew he'd need a hand, so I got up and followed as he took a load out. I heard a lot of noise down the hall, running up and down stairs, but I didn't see anyone. I passed Bob coming back.

"Thanks for cleaning up the kitchen," I said as I zipped down the steps, wondering if there was anyone who could make a bigger mess than Susan. I went outside on the stoop and leaned over to dump the trash. I had an eerie feeling I wasn't alone.

I was right. A big black arm curled around my neck, a knife pressed against my throat. Someone was feeling in my pocket and had my keys. They jiggled in front of my eyes and seemed to be the source of the voice — "Let's just go right back upstairs, man, where you came from."

There were several in the gang, their eyes wild, their hair all raised up like flames.

I didn't see any point in arguing. I had heard about raids of this kind before. Whole flats cleaned out! At the top of the flight, I saw Marty.

"What's the party about?" he joked. Then he saw the knife.

"Just you come along, too," the big guy said.

Marty and I were pushed along to our pad. The junkies slammed the door behind us and forced us into the kitchen, all the time growling, "Someone's got money here. Where is it?"

By now, I was being held up against the wall in the kitchen. The goon was threatening me with his long knife pressed up against my throat. One slip and I could be a statistic. Penny was screaming, "Take your hands off Marty," to the other junkie. Whenever she screamed, the guy holding Marty pushed him even harder.

One of the gang had picked up my wolf parka. Verne had gotten it from an Eskimo during his USO tour in Alaska and had given it to me. It had been my house during the fuel strike. It meant a lot to me. One of the junkies took Marty's watch off and a ring and went out the door. As soon as one of them had carried an armload of stuff out into the hall, he'd reappear for something else, yelling, "Give me, give me."

Right in the very middle of this chaos, Janice staggered in! I felt like welcoming her back from her crime spree! She was drunk and looked as though she had been thoroughly beaten up once already. "Get your hands off my friend!" she screamed at the guy pressing me against the wall. "You let go of him, you s.o.b." She weaved across the room and started beating him on the back.

The junkie snarled, "Get her off me. Tell her to quit or I'll kill ya."

"Yeah, yeah, *okay!* Janice, sweetheart, be nice to the little man. For God's sake, stop it! I want to live!"

But I wished, for once, her friends, Bobby Gillespie and Johnny Machine, had come up with her. Their stubby little gats would have blown some neat holes in a few bodies.

Then I got a bright idea. "Look, fellows," I said. "I'll admit it. I have got some money. Ten bucks. In the other room. If you'll let me go for a minute. . ."

The guy breathed his foul breath in my face, then released his hold on me. I was free! For a moment.

I headed for the room Lucky was sleeping in. I closed the door behind me. "Lucky! The junkies are here. They're ripping off the pad. Our stuff is going out like bargain day at Bekins. Come on, get up, do something. Help us."

But Lucky opened one eye, didn't seem to like what he saw, closed it again, rolled over and went back to sleep.

When I opened the door that led into the long hall, Susan's dog, Brandy, scooted out in front of me. He dashed ahead, into the living room, yapping and snapping. Everyone was screaming, and the dog was jumping around and nipping at the junkies.

Meanwhile, the big guy, the ringleader, was leaping around trying to keep away from Brandy's fangs. "Get him outta here," he shouted, "or I'll kill him."

IT'S GOOD TO KNOW

"You kill that dog, and I'll slaughter you!" I screamed. "You guys get out of here. Now! Or I'll kill you!"

A couple of them looked at me as though I was out of my mind. But I looked right back. I was freaked out of my mind! I was suddenly deathly sick of the whole rotten mess . . . sick of being kicked around . . . sick of everything I had done and what had been done to me. I was ready for murder, suicide, anything.

The ringleader kept staring at my eyes. I had a strange feeling that suddenly he had recognized something in someone else's eyes that was as evil as he was.

"Ah, this place is a drag. Let's split." He took off. The others, loaded with souvenirs, trailed behind him, like ugly ducklings after their black mother.

In a morbid sort of way, I felt better. But I had another strange sensation: I wondered if this was the end of my troubles — or just the beginning.

Lucky, finally fully awake, came out of hiding just as they left. We all ran out into the hall and downstairs to see which way they were headed. No trace. They'd melted into the city like magic. No one was on the street except the whore who always hung out in the doorway across from us. She waved and smiled.

When we got back to the pad, the girls were screaming. Janice was jabbering like an idiot. Bob was moaning. No one was making sense. I just stood in the middle of the room. "Stop! And get out of here." I pointed to Marty and Penny. "You two, get to bed."

The two drop-in girlfriends split. I turned to Bob. "Why don't you find a place to stay?"

"Yeah, yeah. Give me a couple of days," he said, shaken up, first by the junkies, then by me.

Even Lucky offered to go.

After everyone disappeared, I tried to talk to Janice, but she wasn't rational. I just said, "In the morning, you split, too. I thought you were gone for good and I promised the pad to Susan. We don't need any depressed alcoholic Bonnies around here."

She looked at me with her bloodshot eyes and slurred, "Ya can't kick me outta my own pad." Then she passed out. I straightened her out on the rug and went to bed.

Everything was quiet and I was ready to call it a night when Janice woke up again. She came up fighting. She stumbled into the kitchen grabbed some plates and started throwing them against the wall, screaming, "So, I'm not good enough for you now, eh, Randy? Not good enough for dear little ole Randy anymore. You hear that? I'm no good. . ." She hurled a cup past my ear, I ducked out of the kitchen.

Marty came back out and half-carried her to her old room, now Susan's room, and put her in Susan's bed.

"Listen," I said. "I'm sick of everyone, all these people, like you and Penny and the rest of them, running around like they own the place. I should charge admission!"

I conked out on the couch and the next thing I knew it was 4 a.m. and two women were shrieking their heads off. I ran down the hall to the bedroom.

"Who is this ---?" Susan was back and yelling. "In *my* bed?"

Janice was screaming right back. *"Your* bed? What do you mean, *your* bed?"

"Nice of you to come back," I told Susan coldly. "Janice is right. She's the lady I leased the apartment from. But she'll be leaving in the morning. Let's just get some sleep for now and talk about it tomorrow."

In the morning, I refused to listen to Janice's whining about my having taken over her apartment. I took her down to the bank, gave her some money from what little I had left, and said goodbye.

When I got back to the apartment, I was relieved to see everyone else had taken off. I told Susan not to give me any trouble.

IT'S GOOD TO KNOW

Now that I had flipped my lid and told everyone where to head in, I felt as though I had not only evened the score after the apartment rip-off, but settled a few hashes of long standing. I had the upper hand and I was going to take advantage of it. "You stay cool, Susan," I commanded.

I thought that, with all these other people gone and Susan and I alone again, maybe things would drift back the way they had been.

But for the next few days, we didn't have much time to patch it up. I worked Friday night at the restaurant and by the time I got in, she was asleep. I didn't try to wake her up. She was finally working, too. Penny had gotten her a job in a restaurant and, since she hadn't worked in a while, I knew she was beat.

Saturday and Sunday were hectic . . . people in and out of the place, sloppy, loud, ill-mannered. But they were good tippers. By the time I left the Roast Beef and Brew Sunday night, it was 9 p.m. and in my pocket I had more than $150 in tips from three nights.

My vibes seemed in tune again, and I decided to head for the White Horse for some Kaluha, then maybe even take something home and wake Susan up and have a ball like old times.

I walked out of the restaurant whistling a tune I hadn't even thought of for years. I had been counting on that money to repair my bike. Janice had all but cleaned me out after the rip-off. Then a hand reached out from nowhere, pulled me into an alley and pushed me against the wall. "Can we have some money?"

A knife flashed at my left side and the barrel of a gun on my right.

"Money? No, I have no money for you, pal!"

Then there was that killer question I was afraid they would ask — "Well, can we have all we find on you?" Someone pushed my head up against the wall harder. I could feel the gun climbing to my head nudging my ribs with the nuzzle as it went.

I shrugged. My pockets were loaded and one guy already had my wallet out. Nobody was in sight and I had no way to attract attention without getting my head blown off or my throat slit.

There were five or six of them. They slipped away like ghosts — not leaving me enough bread for the subway.

I backtracked wearily into the restaurant and borrowed a dime.

Now I was pretty sure of the answer to my question — this was just the beginning of trouble.

11

OFF AND ON, I had been working on the riot manual. I'd finally finished the copy and layout and given them to Quicksilver. He said he'd have galley proofs for me soon. In less than two months — May Day!

I started laying tracks to return to Colorado, or maybe go to California, as soon as the big march was over. I'd had New York. I hoped I could get out before something worse happened to me. It seemed to be a race against time...

I didn't seem to be in control of anything. Like riding a bike and being unable to make it do what I wanted it to, the bike going faster and faster, the traffic whirling around me until suddenly, everything comes together and closes in all at once in a wild crash, a crunching, a mangle of blood and metal.

Nothing seemed to be working out. I had been in great shape, yet I couldn't seem to hold onto money that passed through my hands. The rip-offs were only part of the story. Everything seemed to be costing me.

As fast as I made a deal, something happened to cheat me of the profit. Every time I planned to fix up my Triumph so I could ride it again, something happened to the extra money I'd set aside. I had a deal with my boss, Harry Ferguson, to fix up three old bikes at the garage and sell them, in exchange for a beautiful little 100cc Zundapp Road Racing Bike, glittering with all kinds of fancy racing equipment and trick stuff. Harry had acquired it from one of the messengers who owed him money, but the messenger was contesting whether Harry actually owned it or not. Meanwhile, Harry said, "Randy, it's now yours, but you still owe me on it, and it stays here till you pay off the rest."

The mix-up came about because one of the bikes I'd fixed up as part of the deal had fallen apart; the guy who'd bought it was demanding his money back. "We made a deal," I protested. "I can't help what the jock did to it after he bought it."

Nevertheless, Harry figured I owed him some money on the Zundapp. It was locked up in the garage until we settled our dispute. So I was still going to work via the subway and/or bus because I still didn't have my own wheels.

It was a great birthday present. I had planned on that Zundapp as a kind of investment. I would sell it, and with that money, get my Triumph fixed up and still have enough money to pay off people I owed — including, maybe, Master Charge, who had finally traced me in New York and were giving me a hassle.

The rip-offs had been a prelude to a glorious twenty-first birthday, all right. The only real birthday present was being 21 and "free," technically and legally an adult. And, responsible for my own deeds!

Susan forgot my birthday, of course. My reorganization had not changed things after all; she was back to her old tricks and nagging about the apartment. My birthday came and went and I didn't feel any different. I was still just a thin strip of negative space spinning my wheels aimlessly.

In order to get some extra money and try to head off what looked like real disaster, I wheedled my way into the "bonus" run at Cosmic Messengers — and that was part of the reason I didn't just go unlock that Zundapp and take it home and tell Harry to see if he could get it from me. I

IT'S GOOD TO KNOW

needed that big-paying run in order to buy myself a trip ticket. It was just possible that if I ripped off that Zundapp without coming to an agreement with Harry, I might lose it to him, anyway, and then I'd have less than nothing. So I'd play it cool for a while until I was ready to make my grand finale . . . May Day, then bust!

So I became a "fleeter," running the super-super rush-rush jobs. My main customer was the race track. I had to be at the Aquaduct Racing Track at 12:30, wearing a little lapel pin with a special number. I'd rip into the parking area near a particular gate, making a lot of noise, then scream, "Ninety Six!" The doors would open, and I'd be in.

I'd go upstairs to the press box with all the reporters, jive with the people, have lunch, a couple of chicken salads and a beer, maybe. I'd even make a couple of bets. At the end of the first race, the photographers would get their first pictures and rush downstairs to the darkroom. They had a special process to develop the film ultra-fast. They'd make 8x10 prints, several poses, several copies of each pose and put them in special envelopes while they were still wet.

From then on, it was up to me. I shoved the envelopes in my green messenger bag. The trick was to get back to Manhattan before all the afternoon deadlines. It was a mad race through town. I'd have to make seven or eight deliveries to wire services, as well as newspapers, in a couple of hours whatever the weather or traffic.

I'd zap down to Manhattan, via the 34th Street tunnel, hit the New York *Post* first, then a Spanish-language paper nearby. After that, I'd dip over to the New York *Times,* scoot over to Rockefeller Center and drop an envelope at Associated Press. Then I had to whirl over to the East Side to catch UPI. Following this, I visited the Brooklyn paper across the 59th Street bridge and then, maybe, I was finished. All this had to be done by 3 p.m. The killer deadline was the 2:10 at the *Post,* requiring me to go 18 miles in 15 minutes.

Cosmic paid $50 a day for this run because of the heavy

responsibility, the crucial deadlines, the speed demanded, the driving skill necessary. And the hazards.

The race run didn't help my nerves any. I was already thin and gaunt from too much dope and not enough sleep, too much rushing around and hassling with people and too many meals that consisted of gut bombs and scotch.

I tried not to admit it to myself, but I was just about burned out and was hanging on by a thread.

When I got up one morning, I knew it was going to be a lousy day. It started out rainy, wet, and chilly. Foreboding clouds clung just above the tops of the skyscrapers. Susan was a witch, filling my ears with filth. I missed a bus and got to Cosmic late, feeling sick and depressed.

It rained off and on, and in between there was a cold mist. Everyone seemed on edge. I had to go up to Harlem and spent most of the day there on short runs getting in and out of traffic, parking and unparking, getting on and off the bike to deliver messages. In between I had to find phones to call in to see where to go next.

I kept thinking I saw things zooming at me — then fading away. By afternoon, I was in a foul mood. I was dragged out and in a hurry to get home — with the prospect of home itself unpleasant.

I was roaring along at better than 60 on a Honda S-90, in the meat-packing section of Manhattan, on the West Side in the Village. I had taken the 14th Street exit. Suddenly, a car, turning from the traffic lane, loomed up out of nowhere, in front of me. I was cut off! A big drainage ditch on one side of me, a semi-trailer parked ahead. I put the bike into a skid on the wet pavement, but I couldn't avoid him and broadsided the vehicle.

I went flying over the top and saw ground rushing at me. My head hit a light pole, caving my helmet in.

When I finally came to, I was aware of throbbing pain all over. Woozy, I tried to focus my eyes. I had double vision. I saw four white-helmeted men dressed in white with big blotches of blood all over the fronts of their coats. I gasped. I was in heaven. This was the culmination of the strange hallucinogenic visions I'd had this wet, grey day.

I was in some kind of cosmic surgery. I must have really been mangled for there to be that much blood, I thought, looking around at the four and seeing the blood on their coats undulated. No one could lose that much blood and live. I had to be dead.

They started pulling on me. Two or three pairs of hands were pulling at my bashed helmet, at my scuffed green bag, at my clothes. They were tugging at my head. I thought I heard crying and wailing. I wasn't in heaven, after all. I was in red/white/and grey hell, and they were picking me apart.

But then I realized what I had been hearing for about five minutes were sirens, getting closer and closer. Now I knew I wasn't actually dead, after all. Not yet. I focused my eyes a little better and read the letters on the coat of one of the four ... "Something-or-Other Meat Works." I gulped. That explained the white clothes, the blood. I glanced around. I was lying on wet cobblestones.

One of the labeled men said, "Don't try to kid me. You can't be alive. You're dead."

I looked around. I saw the car, with a big dent in its side, the windows cracked ... the bike, twisted front end, handlebars bent ... gloomy facades of buildings.

Then two police cars, sirens dying, skidded to a stop, cops spilled out, an ambulance droned to a stop and the first-aid man hopped out. He examined me quickly. "No bones broken," he reported to one of the cops. "Cuts, bruises, Wrenched back, neck."

"How do you feel?" the cop asked gently.

"I dunno. Okay ... I guess." My head was a bulb of throbbing pain which shot down my back in stabs that took my breath away and made me dizzy. I was nauseated. It was hard to talk, hard to keep my eyes open, hard to stay with it. "I think I've really hurt my back," I managed to squeak.

"Yeah. You screwed up your back muscles, for sure," the first-aid man said.

"But no bones broken," the cop emphasized, with relief.

One of the other policemen had tried my bike. "It's still running..."

All this time, the police car and ambulance radios were blaring away with urgent calls, and one of the other cops or the ambulance driver were constantly interrupting everything to answer calls. "Rip-off on 14th Street...," "Heart attack in Harlem..."

Their attention was also distracted by the driver of the car I had broadsided. He was sitting in his car wringing his hands and looking over at me, then at the cops. The cops were checking distances from the car to the point of collision.

"Think you can make it?" one of the cops asked me, quietly.

I thought of all the bad times I'd given the cops, and the smart talk and the dirty words I'd hurled at them. I moved to get up, and they reached down and helped me to my feet. I started to feel really bad about how I'd felt about cops, and was about to thank them, when the thought came into my mind that they were just pigs doing what they were paid to do. "Yeah, yeah," I said finally. Why the hell should I ask them for any favors? "I'm okay... I'm okay." I struggled over to my bike.

The other cop turned to the ambulance driver. "You'd better go on to that heart attack. We'll follow you in."

I became dimly aware of the driver of the car I'd hit, getting out of his vehicle. Then he was at my side as one of the policemen waited behind while the other took off behind the ambulance. The driver and I exchanged addresses.

I drove slowly to the messenger service and told Lucky what had happened. Everything was a blur. Things started to whirl around me.

When I woke up, I was lying in a hospital bed. "What place is this?" I asked the doctor examining me.

"St. Vincent's."

A man named Stanley, whom I recognized as Cosmic's attorney, materialized beside the doctor. "I got most of the details," he said. He shoved a paper at me. "You want to sign this power of attorney to act in your behalf? They had to cite the other driver for improper turning, and we're going to sue."

Why not? What could I do about it myself? The only insurance I had was through the company, while on duty. Which I had been. Painfully, I leaned over to sign.

"We'll be in touch," the attorney said. "Take it easy." He left.

"No fractures," the doctor said. "That's good. But you're injured."

"Oh."

"We'll have you x-rayed. Just take some of the pills the nurse gives you for pain, and we'll get back to you."

Lucky came to see me and I gave him a message for Susan. He came again the next day, but Susan didn't show up.

In a couple of days, the doctor gave me the results of the x-rays. "You've hurt your neck and spine, and the little cushions between the vertebrae. You can get out in a day or two . . . we can't keep you here. But you had better get yourself over to a specialist . . . Dr. Parks. I'll give you his address. You need to have traction and therapy, if you want to put yourself back together completely."

I grunted. How would I work? What would I do? How would I pay him?

When I finally got home the next day, Susan was having a bite to eat in the kitchen — raisin cake and yogurt.

"Why didn't you visit me at the hospital?" I asked.

"My job. . .," she mumbled.

I didn't press it. It hurt too much just to be awake, without getting excited.

The nurse had given me some pills for pain and sleep, but

I knew of better pain killers, and after resting a while, I went out, even putting up with the elevator to avoid having to ache my way down 12 flights of stairs.

I started out the front door of the building when a short, tangle-haired hippie stopped me on the steps. He looked familiar but I couldn't place him right away, so I started to edge past him, keeping my distance so as not to get bumped.

"Don't you recognize me, Randy? I'm Drake Cummings."

Looking closely, I remembered. He was a guy I had dealt in dope with in Arizona. "Let's sit on the step," I suggested. "I'm hurting."

"I'm splitting right away," he said. "I want to unload some grass. At Arizona prices."

The accident had not only cost me money, but had put me out of circulation as far as making any more was concerned. I made the mistake of nodding. After I'd come down from the wall, I said, "What's the price?" Maybe I could double or triple what money I had left.

"How does 90 bucks a pound grab you?"

I tried to remember what he had been like when I'd known him in Tempe and Scottsdale, and I thought he'd changed, though I couldn't be sure. But he'd always been square, so I thought, "What the heck?" I got up — and said, "Yeah, I can make a bundle all right, and it's just what I need right now."

"Yeah," Drake said, in a more relaxed way. "Sorry about your wreck. I wouldn't give you such a good deal, if you weren't on a bummer like you are. I thought to myself. 'That Randy needs a little help along about now.'"

I took a deep breath. Tears came to my eyes. Other than Lucky's nice words, this was the only other person in town who seemed to feel sorry for me. "Let's go to the bank," I said, "and I'll draw out about $300 or $400. I can double that or better. It's about all I have but I know I can push the stuff easy. The bank's just two or three blocks from here. Easy walking." I groaned. "Or was."

"Yeah, well, you're not going to walk." He yelled for a cab.

After I'd drawn the money out, I handed it to him. He gave me a package. "What's this? I thought you said you had to go back to your hotel. . .?"

"Oh, it's just some pills, for security, you might say."

"You don't have to. . ."

"Well, hell, Randy," he said. "My hotel's clear across town, and you're in no condition to go with me, through all that traffic in one of those maniac cabs, the way they drive."

He got a cab, and I rode as far as my apartment building. "I'll be up in my apartment," I said. "See you in a couple of hours and we can blow some joints, jive, the bit."

"Sure" he said, and he waved good-bye and took off.

I waited the rest of that afternoon, all that night, the next day. I never saw him again. Or my $400.

He'd cleaned me out. And the pills turned out to be dummies. Not for real.

And this was the day I was supposed to see the specialist — who had worse news for me. The total bill would be several thousand. "Don't worry," he said. "Your employer's insurance company is suing. You just have to put $500 down, and we can start a real therapy program for you."

I showed him the lining of my pockets. "I pass," I said, and left.

What next, I wondered, as I took the subway home.

Walking towards the apartment building from the subway exit, I saw a bunch of kids running and yelling. One of the kids had a backpack on his back, and someone else was chasing him, screeching. Two little girls were fighting over a small radio. A kid was showing a portable TV set to his companions. There was a whole mob of them hassling over all this, and I wondered if there had been a riot and more looting. Then I recognized the stuff. "Hey, you brats!" I shouted, trying to wave my arms, and wincing, "That's my junk. Give it to me."

I managed to collect it and put it in a pile by the door. I hired one big guy to guard it for me, then took what I could carry on one trip, and went upstairs. The door to my apartment was locked. I yelled and knocked. Once, twice. Three times. No answer. Susan must be out. I found my key and put it in the lock. It wouldn't work. It wasn't the same lock that had been on the door in the morning.

I banged on the door. "Susan," I yelled. "Susan. I know you're in there. . ." And I banged some more.

Finally, Susan yelled back, "I don't want any. Go away."

I knew it was useless. She'd pitched me out.

"I had the lease signed over to me," she yelled. "Find yourself another pad."

"I'm sick," I said.

"Yeah, you sure are. A sick brain. What good are you to me?"

I knew it was no use. I also knew how she'd gotten the landlord to sign over the lease. I'd seen him leering at her several times. And she had winked back and given him a sweet smile.

I was fed up. I didn't even bother to tell any of my friends what had happened, or that I needed a place to stay. Friends? What were friends? The word had no meaning. There wasn't any such thing.

I did condescend to ask a waitress at the Beef and Brew if she'd keep my stuff.

That night I slept in the subway.

The next day, I phoned Brian Hurst. He had said he would let me share his Wall Street pad for $175 a month. A real classy room. I explained the situation.

"Well, gosh, Randy," he replied, "with your being out of work and no money coming in . . . the reason I considered it in the first place was I'm trying to save up some money to get back into public relations. Another guy has asked if he

Photo — Courtesy of Littleton High School, Littleton, Colorado

Randy Bullock (left), with friend Ed Kane, relax backstage while waiting for their stage cues in a high school production of *Kiss Me kate*.

Photo — Courtesy of the University of Colorado, Boulder

During his first year of college at the University of Colorado in Boulder, Randy Bullock turned to playing roles in social protest plays. In the photo Randy is rehearsing his part as a union boss who is trying to refrain a riot at the union hall in a scene from the play *Waiting for Lefty*.

In New York City, Randy Bullock not only rubbed noses with organized crime as he raced around town as a motorcycle messenger, but also became a law violator as a dope peddler. The photo, taken in 1971, shows Randy in a theatrical disguise while "cutting" three kilos of "grass" having a street value of $2,500.

Randy Bullock (right) spending a recent vacation with his parents at Parker Dam in Arizona.

Randy Bullock, a racing enthusiast, is shown as he rounds a corner during the 50th Annual Pike's Peak Hillclimb in Colorado. Randy won a fifth place trophy in this nationally known racing event.

Photo by John Patrick Prince, Courtesy of World Wide Pictures

A photo of Randy Bullock taken from a scene in the World Wide Pictures film *Isn't It Good to Know*. In this motion picture, Randy tells of his former lifestyle as a radical yippie while living in New York City and Washington, D.C. The film also features Billy Graham.

Photo by Frank Raymond, Courtesy of World Wide Pictures

Randy Bullock (left) as he appeared in a rap session scene in the World Wide Pictures' film *Isn't It Good To Know*. The film won a gold medal at the New York Film Festival and a silver medal at the Atlanta Film Festival. Seated next to Randy are co-stars Kirt Meirike and Linda Martini, the California State Water Skiing Champion.

Photo by Frank Raymond, Courtesy of World Wide Pictures

Standing beside the microphone is Randy Bullock who played the role of a street preacher in the World Wide Pictures' film *Time To Run*. The photo was taken following Randy's message on love to a group of outcast teenagers gathered on a hillside somewhere in southern California.

Photo by Steven R. Gottry, Courtesy of World Wide Pictures

According to officials at World Wide Pictures more than four million Americans have seen *Time To Run* at their local theaters. The publicity photo shows Randy Bullock as he appeared during a six-month nation-wide road tour for World Wide to promote the film. The foreign release of the film is planned soon.

**Photo by Ake Lundberg,
Courtesy of the Billy Graham Evangelistic Association**

Randy Bullock (left) is being introduced by Cliff Barrows at the 1973 Upper Mid-West Billy Graham Crusade in Minneapolis. Randy told the crowd of 35,000 people how a decision for Christ changed his radical yippie life style. Later the Crusade and Randy's testimony were televised on more than 200 stations nationwide to an estimated viewing audience of 20 million people.

can move in. Offered me $200 a month. Listen, old boy, if things were going better for me. . ."

"Okay," I said with final resignation. "Never mind."

"Now, now, hold on there a minute," Hurst said, obviously having a hard time. "This is really terrible, you know. I'd really like to help you. Heck, you can stay with me for a week or two. Till that other guy . . . that'll give you a chance to find a place and get on your feet."

When I got there, I hardly noticed the elegant surroundings. By now I didn't need physiotherapy. I needed a shrink. I was out of my head.

Brian told me the original owner of the Zundapp had ripped it off from the garage. I went to his flat and talked to him. "It was a rip-off in the first place. Harry ripped it off me," he said. "You try to get it back, I'll send the cops after you."

I did try to get it, when he was gone, several times. But he never left it where I could find it, and I was too sick and hurting to keep after it. I had to give up. All the time and money I'd invested in it was gone with the exhaust. And I still owed Harry for it! So he said. I owed Master Charge, everyone.

I had nothing but a broken Triumph, a wrecked back, and a mind that was dissolving.

What else could happen I kept asking myself, over and over again. I'd been ripped off, beat up, had my motorcycle wrecked, my back wrecked.

"Is this what I've lived for?" I asked myself aloud and answered, "What you're seeing is the sum total of your life. You are where you belong. Or, rather, you belong back in the subways because that's exactly what you've earned, exactly the amount of love you've given, and exactly the amount of respect you'll get back."

Why was Brian acting so strangely? Every time he passed my room, he seemed to shudder. Brian, what's eating you? Why are you staring at me? No — no. Don't go . . . why are you backing away? There's nothing wrong with me. It's just the world.

There's a power of evil, a bad vibe, and I'm riding on top of it, heading toward the rocks . . . No, no! I'm not going crazy. It's just everyone else, they're out to get me. All of them. Brian, too. Got to watch them. A man can't be too careful. . .

12

MAY DAY should signify Spring, flower festivals, and rejoicing that the long, hard winter is over. But there were no flower children in New York anymore. No more nice hippies. No one to deliver flowers to your door in a basket on May Day.

But we weren't planning any Spring festival for Washington, D.C. My enthusiasm had waned after the accident, but now I was looking forward to getting out of my particular rat race. "Maybe this will be a new beginning," I thought. "A chance to get back at them. At least, I've got Lucky."

Lucky had bailed me out again. He had come to see me at Brian's. "You've got to get a hold on yourself, Dr. Bullock," he said. "It's bad, sure, but not that bad."

The next day, he brought the galley proofs of the riot manual from Quicksilver. Looking them over and making some corrections helped me to come down from my head spin and patch up the holes, though I kept having relapses, repeating over and over again, "What's the use, what's the use?"

But the prospect of May Day: the change, the excitement, the challenge, and the chance to do what I had come to New York to do in the first place, was good therapy.

Finally, I ventured into the outside world again. Brian was

relieved. He'd been living in terror with me around throwing fits. He was afraid to kick me out, fearing, I guess, that I'd get killed — or kill myself. Or someone else.

Lucky was living with Sissy in one of Joe LeProtto's apartments in Little Italy. He said Joe had another place, on the Lower East Side, for $10 a week.

When I talked to Joe about it, he wasn't the wisecracking safecracker I'd known before. He was curt, mean. "I don't know. You ain't got a job. But, okay . . . but it's a steal at $10 bucks a week, so you better come up with the loot on time every week or you'll be out in the gutter. Get it?"

I got the message, all right. Just what I'd said before: Smile at you when you're in the pink. Kick you in the gut when you're down and out. The human rat race.

But at least I had a place to live.

When I saw it, I thought, "This is living?"

It was a tiny walk-up above a store front, no kitchen, just a room, a john, a sink, a refrigerator. Plaster — filthy, yellowed, and cracked. Two tiny windows looking onto the sooty bricks of a building five feet away, windows with broken glass and tattered, greasy curtains.

Crammed into the rooms on either side of mine, and across the hall, were millions of Chinese — whole families in little cell-like rooms with kids bawling, screaming in Chinese, and running up and down the halls and on the crumbly sidewalk outside. The building, which looked as if it was ready to cave in, was a part of the dregs of the Lower East Side, the Bowery, where winos and bums boozed, staggered, fought, heaved, and died all over the streets day and night.

I moved in. The room seemed like my coffin.

But Lucky kept coming up and talking about May Day and encouraging me to get with it and join the crowd and do something to make everything better, and I tried to square my aching shoulders and face it and pull myself up.

We made another scouting trip to D.C. via Pennsylvania, to his old hometown, and we spent the night there, just walking around and gawking at the town. Lucky told me about his childhood. I had been able to teach him a few things about motorcycles, and now he taught me a few things about orphans.

This was just a little mining town but everyone knew Lucky. People would yell across the street, "Lucky! Hey, how are you?"

By the time we got to D.C., I felt as though Lucky had been my best friend all my life. Except for Brian, who had been afraid of me most of the time and steered clear of me, he had been the only one who had really stuck by me in New York, especially after the accident. I didn't know until that trip why he was so uptight about war. He told me some of his experiences. He'd been a paramedic in the Green Berets. He knew how to work with plastic explosives and a lot about ballistics and arson. I knew he had no fear; I guess that's why I liked to be around him.

We arrived in D.C. in time for the big party that was to take place in Potomac Park. We'd missed the gigantic mass march to the White House steps. Lucky spotted a good place to drop our backpacks and we set up house. Then we looked around. There were backpacks, bedrolls, booze, and girls everywhere. Right next to us, nestled in some trees, were two girls who looked interesting.

"Let's see if we can offer them some grass," I suggested, "Maybe they'll have some extra chow." I could hear a can being opened, and it looked as if they had a good set-up, just as I remembered when we used to camp back home in Colorado. We got acquainted with the two girls, Angie and Priscilla, from Mary Washington College in Fredricksburg, Virginia. Southern girls, all the way!

All night long, people sang songs, played guitars, sat rapt or rapping, discussing philosophy, sex, freedom, peace . . . some just sitting in the blue haze of whatever trip they were on. Lucky and I stuck to grass. We wanted to be ready for the main event next week and we had a few more things to check out for Quicksilver.

The girls promised to meet us the following week in the park in front of the hospital tent, saying they'd bring more wine and food. They didn't have as far to come as we did. I liked Angie, and she seemed to dig me. She had an outdoor look, a refreshing change from what I'd seen in New York.

We took off early in the morning, got a good hitch all the way to New Jersey, and another the rest of the way in, and made it in time for Lucky to be back on the job.

My back was still too hurt to drive that week, but despite our continuing controversy over the Zundapp, Harry and I got together to arrange some garage work. I needed money to live on and also to help finance the big main event, May Day itself. With some of the money, I bought dope and sold lids to increase my nest egg. I even got some H at a cut-rate price to ease my back pain. It seemed almost as if nothing had changed . . . until I'd go home to that rat hole.

One neighbor, Charlie, made it more bearable. He was a cultured, middle-aged Cantonese, down on his luck, but full of Buddha and bright chat. He lived a couple of doors down the hall. "Me flat out, you flat out, okay? Then, chop chop, we get back on our foot, okay? Confucius say, 'Man who smile in dark time like moon lighting up night.' "

That was something to think about. Charlie didn't go for dope. "Me use smoke opium. That why I have scar on cheek. Fight over dope — whop, whop. Flesh cut. Okay?"

The following week, Lucky and I headed toward Pennsylvania again and got a ride as far as Harrisburg. We were waiting there for another ride when a VW pulled up with four passengers, three guys and a girl. Lucky got in front next to the girl. I was shoved in back with a couple of guys and thought I could smell hashish. I made a deal to buy some of it for $25. They let us out on Interstate 95, not far from Baltimore.

IT'S GOOD TO KNOW

We hitched into Baltimore and took the bus for Washington.

On the way to the park, foot traffic was heavy. The whole city looked different. "We're seeing a chain of events," I said. At the park, we looked for our girls. More than 10,000 people were roaming around, a rock band was playing, and this time there were signs of more permanent occupants. It looked like Woodstock West all over again ... tents, lean-tos, litter.

But the faces were different. These were real militants. Renny Davis' gang. There were no yo yo's in evidence. We found the hospital and, nearby, Angie and Priscilla. It was exciting!

Girls dressed in khaki were running around, looking as though they were carrying important messages, but I couldn't get a line on what was going on. Nothing had started yet. According to my op-order, the real blast was supposed to go off tomorrow. Meanwhile, there was to be another swinging party with the rock band going all night. Angie and Priscilla had bought wine and we didn't waste time sampling it. The band played on, but I was played out and crashed early.

In the morning the scene was feverish activity. Red lights were flashing all over the place, cars whizzing up, some of them with loudspeakers. A TV camera crew was moving in.

Lucky woke me and said, "They told the people to get out of the park by 11 o'clock. They revoked the park permit. Those who stay'll be busted."

I looked toward the street again and didn't like what I saw. About 200 police were putting on gas masks and helmets, checking out their equipment. Every other one had a riot stick, tear gas gun, or automatic weapon. Shields were distributed. Police were lining up as far as I could see.

Also, it looked as if the whole Army, Navy, and Air Force

had pulled up just outside the main gate. A huge semi-truck drove into the park and stopped not far from where we were sitting on our bedrolls.

About 400 protesters remained in the park, mostly just sitting there, looking as if they were warming themselves in the sun on an ordinary May Day in any city park. But one hyped-up nymph on a makeshift stand was doing a go-go thing as if in a trance, while someone down below played the guitar slowly.

I looked across the water at the White House and the George Washington Monument. The cherry blossoms were in bloom. I wondered what George would have thought of how his beloved Washington looked now.

Suddenly, I remembered Angie. I had to get her out of there! I hurried to the hospital set-up. She was there, talking to an older woman. I took her hand and we ran back to Lucky. "Grab your stuff. You look nice and straight; they'll let you out." She started to protest. "I can take care of myself," I insisted. "We couldn't get out together. I want to be here to witness it if injustices are done."

She picked up her sleeping bag, and off she went, straight toward the lineup of cops, standing shoulder to shoulder by now.

When I returned to Lucky, he said quietly, "I'm staying, too. This is the people's park."

I hardly heard him. A chill was going through me. I felt lightheaded. My eyes weren't focusing. I wanted to split. I felt sick. Suddenly, I couldn't even remember why I was there!

There was a whiteness in front of my eyes. That often repeated scene from my childhood flashed: my father and I climbing the mountain, standing on the very top, my hand in his. Feeling safe and proud, proud of my dad, proud we'd made it to the top of that 14,000-foot peak. How many kids had dads who would climb to the tops of mountains with them? Feeling like I could fly, feeling free. . .

IT'S GOOD TO KNOW

Then I spaced back in. The law enforcement officers were shouting commands, getting ready.

Why can't I go away from here right now, I thought, and be with my father? Why am I not with him right now? I wish he was here. I felt lost. I was about to be hurt, and I knew I couldn't get out of it. I wanted to be protected. I wanted to say, "Dad, I'm lost. Can you help me? It's too much. I can't handle it."

Then I broke and ran for the porta-john nearby. I went in. Through a crack in the boards I saw the cops moving. There was a crunch on the ground as they made their way from the park entrance, step by step, shoulder to shoulder, heads turning mechanically from one side to the other as they marched in slow motion, faces grim. I took the hashish from my pocket, stuffed it up in the rafters of the porta-john and went back out.

Lucky was in front of me. I reached down and pulled my backpack closer to my feet. I started to say something to Lucky, but just then a TV camera crew pounced on us, shoved a mike in my face.

"What do you think about his whole affair?" a little man with dark hair and a nasal voice said, trying to manuever me in front of the camera.

What do I think? I said to myself. Man, you just can't know what I'm thinking right now. You'd censor me out if you really knew. It's kind of ironic that these freaks here who have been planning all this hate and violence and filth for D.C. for years are now sitting here and are about to use the American system of democracy to justify staying in the park. It's ironic that I've tried out for parts in TV and couldn't even get a two-second spot, not even a commercial, and now you're giving me free coverage!

But, instead, I said, "Quite frankly, I had a nice night's sleep, but I wish I wasn't here right now."

They moved on to more interesting views, like the stand where the girl was still dancing. The camera made a wide sweep around the area, probably trying to show the American TV audience what their beautiful Potomac Park looked like now. The huge oak trees and the weeping willows were bowing in the breeze as if ashamed. The litter and yippies in the park made it look like a part of New York's West Side.

I did a 360-degree turn, and as far as I could see in every direction, there were hundreds of people in white — cops and ambulance people — and red lights flashing. Police everywhere. My back was hurting, my stomach ached. The police were about 15 or 20 feet from Lucky. I couldn't hear a sound. Everybody had their eyes on that little group of people. We were zombies.

Suddenly, I reached down, grabbed my backpack, took one last look at the cops, and, as a second camera crew came between me and the police, I shoved my backpack in front of me and dove under a big semi-trailer.

As I crawled to the other side of the truck, I could hear the crowd come to life with a collective gasp, then screams and a barrage of words that hurt even my ears! There was running, scuffling, groans.

As I stood up, all I saw was a photographer about 50 feet away. I shrugged and began to walk, slowly at first so I wouldn't attract attention. Then when I saw I was free, I started to run — and ran until the pain in my back and neck was too much. I went to the Episcopal Church we had scoped out earlier. A freak near the door said, "Welcome. Come in, Brother."

There were 200 people milling around in the church rec hall and upstairs behind the sanctuary, most of them with sleeping bags nearby. A group had maps and were planning the next day's activities; retaliation against the police action and going ahead with the original intention to immobilize the nation's capitol.

A hard-looking, masculine girl holding a cigarette was sitting on a table which was draped in white silk with an embroidered cross. She was talking to the group, most of whom were sitting on the floor. Her speech was foul-mouthed, her gestures brash. With a sour look on her face, she smashed the butt of her cigarette on the silk burning a hole right through the cross.

"What do you think you're doing?" I stood up and swept the room with my eyes. "What is this, anyway? You ask people to believe in your cause and want Nixon to come over to your ideas, yet you do a rotten thing like that! You want everyone to respect you and your rights and your property..." My voice was loud and shaking. But people only yawned and shrugged and grinned. I saw it was useless.

I was so uptight I had to get out. I went upstairs. I went over to one of the ministers. "Is that what it's all about?" I asked.

"I'm sorry to hear they'd do something like that," he said, after I'd told him why I was upset. "We felt we had to offer our sanctuary for the cause of peace, but I agree, that's carrying it too far. What about you?" He started talking about Jesus and I mentioned that my brother, Verne, was making a name for himself as an evangelistic singer. He said he'd heard of him. "You don't go along with his view on God, then?" he asked.

"I can't believe in a God who would let this war go on," I said. "I can't see God in this space age." I looked around, then shrugged. "I can't see God. I can't touch God. I can't believe in intangibles."

The minister raised his eyebrows. "Oh? Can you see magnetism?"

We were interrupted, but I thought about what he'd said. He seemed to believe what he was saying to me. He knew I'd be gone the next morning. Knew I had no money. I couldn't believe he had any motive for talking to me except a deep, sincere feeling. I thought about it as I tried to sleep that night, curled up in my bedroll, uncomfortable and aching.

At six o'clock the next morning, I got up, rolled up my bedroll, and went out onto the street, thinking I would start looking for Lucky. Everything was grey and dismal. Feelings and thoughts stirred my recent experiences, which, along with the weather, depressed me, and what I saw on my walk only added to it. I seemed to be seeing it with new eyes — the thousands of people who had gathered and were causing sporadic trouble everywhere I looked. It was frightening to walk along the streets and see whole busloads of police. It gave me the jitters. I wanted to be invisible, wanted my long hair suddenly short.

I shivered. What was my part in it . . . now? The incidents at the park and the church were bothering me. I felt on the verge of a change I couldn't define, though I felt all the more alienated, no longer a part of this scene.

I forgot all about what I'd come there for, and about Lucky, and started hitchhiking. I was leaving before the final outcome was clear. Before I was a casualty . . . or something.

Most of the cars leaving Washington heading north that day were in too much of a hurry to stop. Finally one did. And I was dumbfounded. The occupant was a girl, Betty, to whom I had lent an unusual ring with a gold band and a black sapphire stone which Verne had gotten in Thailand. And a Mrs. Tall, who had seemed to be in charge of the hospital and office set-up in the park. I recalled how much it had reminded me, the cluster of tents, off-limit signs and general activity, of an Army HQ area. Mrs. Tall had struck me as being a very wealthy person.

I got in, still not believing the coincidence. I'd thought that ring long gone! As we drove along, we talked. I remembered Mrs. Tall had introduced me to a guy named Bret that time before and had said something about Bret being a paid trouble-maker. Now I asked some more questions, trying to clarify it in my mind, trying to trace the chain of command for this whole protest deal.

It turned out that this Bret was a paid trouble-maker on a high level, one who had a crucial part in diverting police and

IT'S GOOD TO KNOW 119

soldiers away from the Senate building — in preparation for somehow "neutralizing" the U.S. Senate! Did that mean bombing it? The women were too guarded to go into details — they said it was super-super confidential. But they went on to reveal that Bret was being paid by a big rock superstar from England.

This was pretty heavy news. But I was so numb and confused and my responses so slow, I really didn't think much about it.

As they were about to let me out by the Jersey Turnpike, Betty asked, "Can I keep your ring a little longer, Randy?" She looked at my strangely. "I feel like it brings me luck."

"Well, yeah, I guess," I mumbled. "I'd like it back some time, though. Would you give me your address?"

She gave me an address in Laconia, New Hampshire.

After they had driven off, I found out I'd been let out at a bad place. I was too weak to walk much, my back was hurting, I was feeling sick, so I just sat in that one spot. After four hours, I got a ride as far as the Port Authority. As I waited by the airlines terminal for a bus, I glanced over at a newspaper rack. And just about passed out. Staring back at me from a copy of the *New York Times* was ... Randy Bullock!! My picture on the front page! Actually, it was a photo taken the day before — snapped precisely the moment of my escape from under the truck. Lucky was in the picture too. But he was clubbed and arrested moments later. And I, moments later, was free!

Just what I need right now I thought. Especially after chucking the whole thing! I was even sicker than I had been. Deep in the head. Back of the eyes. I didn't want to look at that picture, but it held me in morbid fascination.

I finally caught a bus and headed for my apartment.

By the time Lucky got out of jail and back to New York, I had discovered I was suffering from lice. I also needed a shot of H badly because of the pain in my back. And I was out of money.

Lucky was uptight about my leaving Washington in such a hurry. He didn't know I'd looked for him, and he wasn't very convinced when I tried to tell him what had happened. He was shocked at my appearance. "You'd better pull yourself together, man," he said, shaking his head. "You're nothing but skin and bones and your eyes are practically sunk in your head." But there wasn't much he could do for me, and when he left, I felt let down. Lucky had been the best friend I'd had.

What had seemed before like a geographically small town now seemed vast. Now that I had no transportation, and no money for fares. I borrowed Lucky's Honda 100 one day and drove across to get the rest of my clothes from Susan. I hadn't seen her since before May Day. She was rather cool at first, then offered me a beer.

Susan disappeared, and she came back out with a grin on her face. She was bare chested. "See?" she said as she posed in front of me.

"I see you had that plastic surgery done you were talking about," I said dryly. It certainly made her look bigger.

I could tell she wanted to have sex. Suddenly, I snickered. I could give her a nice case of crabs!

But not right now. I had to get the Honda back. And I wanted it to be on my own terms, not Susan's.

I came back that night, and she was all romance. It was hard to realize that this was the same person I'd had all those foul arguments and bad words and hate sessions with. What had happened to her?

We both spaced out on an "I am a nothing human being" marijuana trip, the grass heightening my acute depression until I wanted to scream. But I turned on the radio, and of all things, "Amazing Grace" was playing. It sent chills down my spine. The words got to me —

Amazing Grace, how sweet the sound
That saved a wretch like me,

IT'S GOOD TO KNOW

> I once was lost but now am found
> Was blind but now I see.

I thought, if I'm so brilliant and intellectual, why am I so lost right now? What am I blind to? Is it because of God? I thought about Verne, and I kept flashing off and on that I was destined to become a Christian, too. I even had a vision of him and me together on a rostrum somewhere, and we were both speaking about Jesus.

Then I came out of it and laughed. Fat chance! It was Susan I was with, and we were on the couch. She pulled me down and held her arms around my neck. I remembered about wanting to give her crabs.

In the morning, I woke up to find her still sleeping next to me. I stared at her and was so empty I couldn't feel. I was sick and hungry. Sick of dope. I wouldn't have been able to tell anybody who I was or where I was. I realized then that having a sexual relationship without love was nowhere. Love is harder. I knew I didn't love Susan and never had. What had May Day been? A fizzle. Just like Susan.

Gazing at her naked body with the oversized breasts, I knew she was the most evil thing I had ever seen. And I knew this was the worst feeling a person could have for anyone, namely that you couldn't trust them no matter what they did. Not for a hundred years could I trust Susan. I hated her. I couldn't get out fast enough. I started to walk out. She got up and put on her robe. "Stay, Randy," she said sweetly. "Stay here with me. We can make a go of it. All the problems we had, they were caused by the others..."

"Get out of my way," I growled.

Susan stood in front of the door, hands outreaching, determined to stop me, keep me there. I seized her roughly under the armpits and lifted her off her feet, moved her away from the door, then thrust her hard against the wall, shaking her at the same time.

"Damn you, damn you, damn you!" I screamed, completely out of control. "You sleazy bitch. I could kill you!"

She fell forward slightly toward me, and I banged her against the wall again, harder. Her head hit the wall and hung limply to one side. I let go and started for the door. She slid slowly down the wall, as though lifeless — like a sack of potatoes settling to the floor.

I tore the door open and started to go out. It was dead quiet except for my own noise. What if I did kill her? I thought. I stopped, turned, looked down. She lay in a cool pool of silence. Was she still alive? I looked closely — and noticed she was breathing, her lips trembling.

I slammed the door behind me, so shaky I could hardly stand up. But I took every other step, hanging onto the railing, and made it downstairs fast.

I didn't stop hurrying until I reached my cruddy little hole in the wall. Then I heaved. As I sat on the floor, sick — all at once I realized I didn't have a friend in the world. The last time I'd written my parents, I'd told them I was in Philadelphia. Now I was in total despair, the kind you get when you look around and discover that nobody cares whether you live or die.

My back was killing me, as painful as if the accident had just happened. I went and begged some heroin off a guy that was going to kick the habit. I shot that, but I was so shaky I made jagged holes in my arm. And, after that . . . for a week, I just stayed inside, not really wanting to live any longer. I lay on the floor most of the time. Why eat, anyway? I lay there, as day and then night slowly revolved around me, and sounds, muffled by the walls, seemed to come from some other world, a world I was leaving.

I was itching like murder from the crabs, but I didn't care. So what? When I died, they'd die, too. I only hoped it would be soon. But at other times, everything around me frightened me. At times I was in terror that the rats or the cockroaches wouldn't wait until I was dead, but would start to work on me while I was still alive but too weak to move. I

IT'S GOOD TO KNOW

stared dumbly at the tiny lice, they became giant lobsters pincering away at me.

And sure enough, after a few more days, I could hardly move. I smelled something awful. But I was too weak to do anything about it. I knew I was close to death, as though it was on the other side of the thin wall. Only my skin stretched between me and death.

The last experience, I thought. I had no more thresholds left — except death's.

I smiled. Another first for Randy Bullock! I'll just lie here and watch myself die. I want to know all about it. I want to know how I'll feel, what I'll do. I want to take it all in. I want to know the exact feeling of dying.

Another day came . . . and went.

Morning. Muffled street noises from that other world, the one I was leaving. Just a few more hours . . . maybe even just minutes. I . . . can . . . hardly even roll over.

Bells were ringing, I guffawed. It's getting closer.

Vaguely, then, I heard a commotion outside my door. Someone knocked. Death? They knocked again. "It for you, Misser Bowrock. Telephone. For you." He kept repeating it in a sing-song voice — "For you . . . for you."

That was crazy. That telephone in the hall no longer worked. A gun had gone off in the building several weeks ago, and a slug had hit it.

"It for you . . . it for you."

I dragged myself off the floor. I stumbled, leaned on the door, then opened it. I staggered out into the hall.

The Chinaman was looking at it, at the phone. He was shaking his head. Saying something in Chinese. I had to lean one shoulder against the wall to stay on my feet. I picked up the receiver. "Yeah?"

It was Verne.

13

I FELT COLD all over. Frightened, I hadn't heard from him in months. Then no sooner do I decide to watch myself die than he calls. On a phone that doesn't work. It was dark and deathly quiet in the hall. The usual racket of kids running and of adults stomping and slamming doors was absent. Those on the scene had gathered around me to witness the broken phone suddenly come to life.

"H-how did you get my number?" I stammered.

There was a pause. "We have our ways. How are you, anyway?"

"Lousy."

"We were afraid you might already have left for work. . ."

"Don't have a job anymore. Had a crash. . ." My voice sounded as though it was coming from the bottom of a well and undoubtedly conveyed much more than the words. But part of the reason was that I felt overwhelmed — overwhelmed by the sensation of a presence of a power of unbelievable magnitude.

"Well, we were out here in Wichita wondering how your life was, and —"

"Who's we?"

"Me and my Christian friends," Verne answered. "Don Williams, Dave Anderson . . . about eighteen others." He

IT'S GOOD TO KNOW

paused, then laughed. "It's like this — Dr. Hartman's Wichita Council for Drug Abuse heard our group had helped a lot of drug abusers through prayer and counseling, so they invited us out here. We set up a convention called 'Five Days in June.' Anyway, there's going to be a lot of solid Jesus Rock music — entertainment. It's all going to happen in a giant new convention center called Century Two. . ."

"Don Williams? The guy who started the Salt Company?" I said.

"Yeah, in California. That's where I've been."

The literature Verne and my mother sent had told me something about Don Williams. A guy had turned him on to Bob Dylan, and that experience led to the birth of the Salt Company, a Christian coffee house emphasizing music and operating through Hollywood Presbyterian Church.

The last *Speak Out* newspaper they'd sent me indicated the Salt Company had formed several houses to take people off the streets and give them places to stay.

"Anyway," Verne continued, "we were all sitting around here praying and we decided we wanted you out here in Wichita for this convention."

My heart jumped. This was love! Nobody had acted as though they cared whether I lived or died, and here was love suddenly jangling the phone. It would be impossible to refuse. I wasn't going to say anything mean or offensive to Christians, despite my attitude towards God. For all I knew, it could be God, after all — after all my doubts and bad words. Anyhow, you don't talk back to love. Even so, I did wonder what made Verne think I would suddenly accept such an invitation, knowing how I felt about Christianity.

It was as though he was reading my thoughts — "As we were praying, we felt you would be ready for a change of scenery, a chance for you and me to see each other. You can meet Don. . ."

"I'd like to hear you sing," I said.

"You'll find a ticket at LaGuardia Airport. Your name will

be on it." He laughed. "The plane leaves tomorrow afternoon."

And that was it, I was in a daze. And gradually it dawned on me that my back no longer hurt. Which was impossible, because it had grown steadily worse since the accident. But now it didn't hurt at all. I was hardly aware of what else was said or what happened the rest of the day. It was such a tremendous thing that was happening to me — like being swept up by some powerful force — bodily and spiritually moved.

I bummed three dollars to get to the airport. Once aboard the plane, I was jittery. The thought uppermost in my mind was getting the chance to hear my brother sing. I had always been Verne's number one fan and always loved his music. And now — now I wanted to hear him sing for Jesus.

As the plane lifted above the city, tops of the skyscrapers poking through the muck, I fought to forget what had happened. But the thought of Jesus songs conjured up a vision of the Cross, and seeing the Cross in my mind recalled the scene in the Episcopal Church near the White House the night I had escaped from Potomac Park.

Then thinking about my last few weeks on the East Coast made me all the more anxious to meet the Christian group. How strange the way they had suddenly intersected my life, when that life seemed to be coming to a grinding halt.

The New York people I had met — and finally, the radicals, had done nothing except leave me a hopeless wreck suffering worthless pain. And now here I was, flying in the air with that feeling of being free again.

If Jesus Christ was whom He claimed to be, I would be able to tell by listening to Verne's singing. If all went well, I would arrive in Wichita in time for the kick-off that evening of June 1st.

All did not go well. The plane broke down in Chicago. I had to wait three hours. I was beginning to hurt again, and I wanted some dope. The last few weeks had shown me how dependent I now was on dope, how uptight I felt when I couldn't get it, when I had no money. I needed something to wake me up in the morning, something to keep me going during the day, something to relax me, and a downer to put me to sleep at night.

I hadn't slept well for a long time. The last few days in my rat-hole, lying on the floor, was a taste of hell. I kept thinking about it as we finally soared over green fields below, and the bright blue sky of approaching summer enclosed the plane.

Verne made his way through the crowd as I entered the terminal. "Hello, brother," he said as he put his arm around me. "It's good to see you!"

"Same here, man," I mumbled. I felt humbled, yet uplifted to giddy heights. I had to bite my lip to keep from crying. He looked at me. "Do you want to go on to the house and just rest?"

"House?"

"Yeah. The people here who asked us to come provided a house for us to stay in."

"Well, where's the action?" I asked. "I'd like to go to where it's happening."

"Well, it'll be almost over by the time we get there, but we'll check it out anyway," Verne said. "Wait till you see the new convention center. It's out of this world."

The vast Century Two Convention Center was a magnificent modern edifice, all gleam and glass. We walked up the steps. We could hear music and joyous singing as we stepped through big doors into a huge auditorium. There must have been several thousand people standing, swaying as they sang the haunting Christian folksong, "We are one in the spirit, we are one in the Lord."

It hit me hard. These people — a lot of them young and long-haired, like me, except all shining-faced and happy —

were pointing towards the sky, as they sang the last line, "And they'll know we are Christians by our love." The irony struck me — just about a month ago I'd been in with another bunch of young people raising their fists up in the air, and yelling their hatred of everything. Here was a group of people who seemed to have a sense of brotherhood and love that I could not even begin to comprehend or explain. And suddenly, I wanted it, and wished the session was just beginning, instead of ending.

Verne drove me to the house on Fountain Street which had been designated for the use of the "Committee" from California. It was a large, two-story, old-fashioned frame house, well maintained and with a spacious yard and big front porch.

Verne showed me to a bedroom upstairs where several beds had been placed, and I went back down with him and sat in the living room. Other leaders of Five Days in June came through to go to their rooms or paused to talk with each other. There was a dentist named Biff Oliver; John Block, a professional basketball player from San Diego; Dave Anderson, founder of Lutheran Youth Alive Ministries; Dennis and Danny Agajanian, nephews of J.C. Agajanian, famous race-car driver; and a dozen or so others — professional people, artists, musicians, even former drug freaks, all united in their cause for Christ.

It turned out that Devon Hartman's father had conceived the idea of inviting the group from California after hearing his son describe the work Don Williams and his people were doing on the West Coast. Devon was the fellow who had hitchhiked with Verne to Colorado, the time Ed Kane and I had picked them up in Colorado Springs to bring them home. That was the time when Verne first told us he was a believer, and Ed and I had given him a rough time.

I was in a daze. I was extremely self-conscious because of the needle tracks on my arms, which I kept covered by wearing a long-sleeved shirt. And I was weak — my back

IT'S GOOD TO KNOW

hurt and my neck was stiff. I was debilitated, hungry, run-down, unnerved from lack of dope, and totally exhausted from the sudden changes and activity right after all those days and nights of deathlike torpor in the rat-hole.

But I was also keyed up by the demonstration of love in motion, so much that even when everyone else went to their bedrooms, including Verne, I didn't want it to end. I sat there in the living room a long time, thinking, basking in the warmth and love left behind by the occupants of the room.

Then one of the men came back into the room and sat across from me. He was Peter Frankovich of Columbia Pictures.

"Your brother was telling me about you, Randy," Frankovich said. "Told me about you liking motorcycles and being interested in drama. Where is it with you in life?"

I laughed dryly. "I wouldn't know where to begin telling you where it's at in my life," I said. "But maybe you could tell me how I could keep going straight ahead? Every time I decide I'm going to do something, problems occur and I wonder if it's the right thing or not. I get second thoughts..."

"Second thoughts are the result of not having the right first thought."

"What's that?" I asked.

"The right first thought is Jesus, Randy. Until we put Him first, we never feel sure about everything that comes thereafter. In Matthew 6:33, it says, 'But seek ye first His kingdom and His righteousness...'"

He'd gotten me started. I was so tired I hardly knew what I was saying, but I laid out to him problem after problem. From time to time, he would stop me and summarize, then show me how Jesus could solve that problem or make me able to solve it myself. It seemed there wasn't a problem I could name that Jesus could not solve.

He smiled. "Most of your problems are basically products of fear. Do you know the song, 'Amazing Grace?'"

My spine tingled because that song, that last day with Susan, had triggered the same spooky feeling I had now.

Was I lost, because I did not have God? Was I blind? At that time I had had a visual picture of Verne and the idea of being a Christian someday, as well as testifying on the same platform with Verne!

And now . . . it was uncanny!

I flashed to the present, focused on Peter Frankovich sitting across from me, hearing him say that all my problems were the products of my fears . . . "Randy," he said quietly, "you'll never be completely without fear until you eradicate the fear of your own demise."

"How?"

"Through Jesus Christ. You can do that with Him, because He gives life — eternal life. In John 11:25-26, Jesus says, 'I am the resurrection, and the life; he that believeth on me, though he die, yet shall he live; and whosoever believeth on me shall never die. . .' "

The coincidence of the song being mentioned, along with everything else that had occurred since my arrival in Wichita, convinced me that this whole chain of events leading to this very minute in the living room of 442 Fountain Street had been guided by the Lord.

We talked a little while after that, then I went upstairs and flopped — on a real bed with clean sheets and soft pillows. Despite not taking anything to send me off, I managed to sleep a little better than usual and woke up only a few times when the recurring pain in my back or the itching made me uncomfortable.

The next morning I didn't feel much different physically from a hundred other mornings during the past few months, but I felt strange mentally. I looked in the mirror and was shocked at my pale complexion. I needed to get outside.

After breakfast in the kitchen, and after most of the household had left for planned morning activities and meetings, I went out on the porch to sit in the sun. When Verne

IT'S GOOD TO KNOW

and several people came out on the porch and started singing songs, I knew I wanted to talk to Verne. I asked, "Can I talk to you inside for a minute?"

We went inside, and I asked him something about strumming. He explained and demonstrated, then handed me the guitar, and I tried. I never did say anything important, because when I handed the guitar back to him, he was still full of music and decided to play and sing something which, it turned out, did relate to my concerns.

With his soft western twang, he played, "Jesus' Style*," written by Bob Marlowe. From the beginning of the song I was entranced with his singing. At one point, the lyrics went, "Gonna change your heart/Gonna make you smile/ That's Jesus' style."

This was the first time it occurred to me that Jesus was a "heart" trip. Jesus didn't care about your head at all! Up to now, I had always been trying to disprove a living, risen Savior intellectually, using logical arguments and facts to knock down whatever may have been said about Christianity. The people I had been associated with were always saying, "What's on your head, man?" or "Where's your head?" or "Get into his head."

All our emphasis had been on mind power and intellectual insight. I had never once considered that maybe my entire basis was off. No one, nor any cosmic philosophy, or anyone in church had ever presented me with the idea of Christ being an affair of the heart — Christ being a love affair. Now I thought, "There's style for you! Changing a person's heart, his style, his grace," I suddenly realized that to change society, to change war to peace, hate to love, you had to get into people's hearts. It had to work from the inside out, had to have an inner beginning to stop war and hate. To achieve social as well as military peace, we had to get to the heart of the matter. To be at peace with each other, we had to be at peace with God.

There were tears in my eyes as Verne finished his song,

and I no longer felt a strong need to talk to him. Somehow, we had communicated on a deeper level, from heart to heart. Then someone needed Verne elsewhere, and I was left alone for the rest of the day. But not quite alone.

I looked forward to that night's meeting at Century Two with wild enthusiasm. I felt that Verne had presented me with only a prelude to further enlightment. I was so elated, I was hardly aware of anything else that happened that day and only "came to" when I had seated myself in the vast auditorium. My eyes followed Don Williams as he came up on stage, took the mike, and started talking.

Despite the spell that had descended over me, I realized as I sat there that inwardly a fair-sized part of me was still resisting. I threw out an unspoken challenge to the man standing on stage: "What have you got to say to me?"

Oh, I knew and respected Don Williams. I watched him as he wound up and got into his topic, and my heart ran a little faster, as something radiated from this man. He had a sweet, easy way about him that just took me away and gave me immediate and complete trust. He seemed completely honest.

When he smiled, his smile was a source of light, and each time he made a point, he smiled. He was so friendly, kind, gracious — an extremely together human being. He had a funny way of sitting on his Bible on that high stool on the stage. When he needed it, he'd reach under him, lift up, take it and flip immediately to where he wanted, read a few lines, then put it under him again.

Thinking of him and the spirit of love and brotherhood in that auditorium, I had increased respect for the love of real Christians for each other and humanity. Five Days in June was a demonstration of the unconditional love that Don was talking about.

The twenty who had come out here to Kansas from

IT'S GOOD TO KNOW

California had done so at their own expense, providing their own transportation and meals en route. The people of Wichita had opened up to them, given them the house on Fountain Street to bed down in, put food in that house — breakfast, lunch, and dinner. All over town, marquees exhorted — "Go to Five Days in June! Take your kids. Take your family. Learn where it's at!" Love — everywhere.

All this I now knew in my heart. But something in my head fought on, I still wanted Don to say something to me that would relate to me. I was only one of thousands there, but I knew he had to speak to each of us as individuals, and I was concerned only with myself at this yearning, aching time. Selfishly, I demanded that he succeed in getting under my skin, into my heart.

As I listened, he did begin to get to me. "Unconditional love!" Don burst out. "That's what Christ offers. He doesn't say 'I love you, but' or 'I love you, if.' He says 'I love you, period.' He offers all of you people love. If He can't live up to His claims, He isn't the Son of God. If He can . . . if He can, He surely is God's Son.

"In Ephesians it says God's love passes knowledge and this is comparable to Philippians, Chapter 4:7, where it says "The peace of God, which passes all understanding, shall guard your heart and your thoughts in Jesus Christ!"

"Love," Don continued, "is giving, not taking. Peace. Inside and out. The only love is God's love! You can say you love, but it won't be *love* unless it comes through Jesus Christ!"

I was stunned. This was a major point with me, that nobody else but God is love.

"You can't expect love from a clenched fist. . ."

What God was doing to me, I thought, was taking that fist out of the air, holding it out in front of me, palm up, and saying, "I love you."

I went home that night again in a trance. This was beginning to be Five *Daze* in June!

The third morning, I awoke feeling a little better physically, feeling my heart beating strongly. At breakfast, I talked to John Block, pro-basketball player from San Diego. I told him I needed some physical exercise to go along with the spiritual exercise. "I'm going to work out at the Y in a couple of hours," he said. "Why don't you come down?"

I agreed. Verne said, "Let's drive downtown and see if we can get some tennis shoes."

We got into Verne's red VW and went shopping. Neither of us had much money and it took some time to find a pair of tennis shoes within my budget. We went to a used clothing store and found a pair of trunks that cost a nickel! Then we checked in at the YMCA.

When I got on the court, I found my spirit was a lot more willing than my flesh. John could sink baskets from behind the circle in the center of the floor, a long half-court shot. I tried to keep up, but after about three minutes I thought I'd die. I couldn't raise my arms, and I was self-conscious about the needle tracks, exposed by my T-shirt for everyone to see. My back hurt like blue blazes. Still, I gave it everything I could.

This was the first healthy thing I had done in a long time, and it hurt, but it felt good.

When I got back to the house that afternoon, I found everyone had gone. I was glad. The reaction to the basketball game — and to the three days in June — had set in. I sat in the bedroom alone. I kept catching myself wishing for dope. The physical activity had started my blood moving again, and it was bringing back reports to my brain of the various pain spots, the aches and the fleshly hungers.

Alone, I didn't have the inspiration of love these people had radiated nor the conversation and activities to distract me from myself. Still, their fellowship had left tracks in my spirit. I fought off the physical pains and urgings and doggedly used my heart to think for a change. I decided that there were only three things I wanted, and if God was Who

IT'S GOOD TO KNOW 135

He claimed to be, then these three things could most certainly be mine: I wanted to clean up my "act," body and soul; I wanted a good night's sleep without dope; and I wanted — suddenly, tears came to my eyes — I wanted to be able to tell my father I loved him.

Suddenly I saw that all the hate I'd felt for society was actually an expansion of the hate I thought I felt for my father. And now I knew! It was a phony hate. I remembered I had never felt this hate until my first LSD trip. Then something else came to me — I had felt love for dad, both before and after that trip, even when I was saying I hated him. I felt it, yet I had never told my father I loved him!

I dozed and dazed the rest of that afternoon, then went with Verne to the evening meeting. The main things I got from the meeting were impressions — of love, joy, peace. I really was thinking from the heart now. My LSD-freaked-out memory didn't record much of the events and words, except to note the usual flowing to the front of people who were saved and were invited to come up and receive Jesus Christ as their Lord and Savior.

I was standing there swaying as music was playing; I started crying. I knew the guy next to me was noticing, but I didn't care.

When the meeting broke up, Verne motioned to me "Hey, let's go through the backstage area and check out this theater," he whispered.

The theater was fantastic, rivaling anything I had ever seen. It had a high balcony with steep seats rising up from the center, and it was a theater any actor would give his eye teeth to play in. It was ghostly now in the dim light of the footlights.

Verne and I sat on the stage, and I started to cry again.

"I knew you were hurting," he said.

"Right now, more than anything," I managed to say, "I'd like to hear you sing about God." I remembered that on my way to Wichita, I had told myself that if I could hear Verne sing about God, I would be absolutely certain that God was for real. I'd know it in my blood, somehow.

Anyway, he went to the piano on the stage, and I walked off. I went up the balcony steps as he warmed up on the piano, trying to find something he wanted to play. Then I was up high, looking way down at Verne in the spot of a tiny light playing on him.

What followed was amazing. Verne was a guitarist, not a pianist. Yet, that night he really played the piano! His fingers seemed to dance over the keyboard. Then he sang — making up the lyrics as he played! He had been unable to find a piece in the songs he knew that pertained to the exact moment, so he made up words, words about brothers and families and God. They fit right in with my earlier thoughts about wanting to tell my father I loved him.

Verne had that talent, the rare ability to play a blues rip on the guitar and make up lyrics to go with it right on the spot. Now he was doing it with the piano, composing lyrics that had to do with brothers and families. It was highly emotional.

When he finished, we left the convention center and returned to the house. Verne went upstairs to bed, but I had the feeling that there was one other, very important thing that had to happen tonight. I was drawn back downstairs.

Since hearing Verne sing, I'd been fighting a resentment against having my emotions triggered as they had been today. I still didn't want to give up my head trip, didn't want to accept God on emotion alone.

Downstairs, I tinkered with Verne's guitar for a while, then went out onto the porch. I was alone and the warm night and the stars formed an envelope.

Suddenly, I found myself on my knees: "Jesus Christ!" I moaned. "I want you. I want you to come into my heart. Now."

I'd done it! I'd actually asked Christ into my heart! I'd

IT'S GOOD TO KNOW

asked Him to change my heart! At last I had expressed a feeling that had been teasing the edges of my being these last two days.

Right in the middle of this prayer, a second voice was nagging at me . . . a cry for heroin! It was a moment of heightened sensations as well as deep emotion, and I was aware of the lice itching, my back pulsating in pain, and of the needle marks tickling my arms, as though something inside me was trying to distract me from my communion with God. In another sense, it was as if my whole self was being exposed right there on the porch, the essence of the dirty thing I had become now dragged out and looked at — right in the middle of a prayer for Jesus to accept me!

"God!" I cried, "I can't imagine you living in a body that's occupied by dope. A body that's been messed up, crawling with lice picked up in a cesspool of sin. Do you know what I mean, Lord?

"I pray for a good night's sleep, tonight, Jesus. And, Lord, give me the ability to say to my father, 'I love you.' "

I sighed. There wasn't anymore I could do now that I'd handed everything over to God. I felt spaced out, light-headed, as though my feet weren't touching the ground. But there was no flash of white light, no visions. Just serenity. I had offered myself, that was the important thing.

I got off my knees, went into the house, and upstairs to bed. And slept like a lamb.

---

*Jesus' Style by Bob Marlowe. Copyright 1970.

14

THE NEXT MORNING the bedroom was full of sunshine and hope. I had slept a whole night through. I lay there in my nice, comfortable bed for a few minutes, enjoying the feel of clean sheets.

A loud clanging was going on downstairs, cheerful voices were calling back and forth. I reached up to pull back the curtains, to look out on this glorious new day. As I did so, my eyeballs nearly came out of their sockets! The needle marks, which had looked like miniature birds' footprints on my arms, had vanished! *Impossible!* But they were gone.

Something else occurred to me! I wasn't itching. I couldn't find a louse on me.

I jumped out of bed and started for the door — and had the startling realization that, when I'd hit the floor like that, my back hadn't ached! "What's going on?" I wanted to shout, I glanced in the mirror. Yes, this was me, all right, still looking a little pale, my long hair tangled. I ran a comb through it, pulled on my jeans and a clean shirt, and ran downstairs looking for my brother. "Verne! Verne!" I shouted. I had to show him. I wanted him to be the first to know. I ran into Devon Hartman.

"Well, you're up early," Devon said from a corner of the porch.

IT'S GOOD TO KNOW

"Look, Devon — how does this grab ya?" I shoved both arms in front of him. "He answered two parts of my prayer — two parts, Devon. Can you imagine?"

"Hey, now, hang on a minute, old buddy. I can't see what you're rapping about if you don't stand still." Devon looked at my arms. Then he studied my smiling face. He just said very softly, "Praise the Lord."

I don't remember what happened the rest of the day. I found my brother and talked for a while, and it was as normal and natural as if we had done this all our lives. I wasn't uptight anymore about anything. Instead, I felt big and light with overflowing awe and wonder.

"Maybe God answered more than one prayer last night, Randy," Verne drawled. "You know, I was feeling out of it lately. But I felt so strongly you were ready to accept Jesus, I put in a good word for you last night, too." He grinned. "Reckon I'll be ready to sing again now."

The two of us kind of floated around that day, helping here and there with meetings, witnessing to kids who needed help and wanted their questions answered. I was still shy about saying too much to total strangers, and as the day wore on, I started thinking about New York. "I've got to go back to New York, Verne," I said that night after an especially long prayer at the meeting.

"But Rand, you just got saved. You don't want to go back to that mess. Leave it alone. Come to California with me and start a new life. Whatever there is in New York, it isn't worth going back to."

But I knew I had to go back and say goodbye. I hadn't really left there, yet. I had that bike to do something about, a few things left, like my TV, a radio, typewriter, some clothes. Not much, but all I had. I wanted some addresses of people like Lucky and Brian. With a better perspective, now, I saw as imaginery my feeling that everyone had turned against me.

Verne knew me. He could tell I had to do this. "What'll you use for money? Why don't you ask Dad for a loan?"

"Yeah. All I need is a plane ticket and some cash for eating . . . shouldn't take much."

We got Dad on the horn. When I explained what had happened, he was happily flabbergasted. It was great to talk to him again, and to have this barrier of hate, alienation, and shame lifted. I couldn't say all I wanted to over the phone. "I'll be home soon," I promised and hung up. And not long after, the money I needed came by wire.

The fifth day was sunny and warm. Everyone was looking forward to a big steak fry. We rode in a truck singing and laughing along the way, getting to a ranch dusty and hungry. After a huge steak barbecue during which we praised God for the Five Days in June, we sat around and talked.

Dave Anderson got up and motioned toward me. "See those railroad tracks over there? Like to walk down them a ways?"

I nodded. I hadn't eaten like that since going camping with my father. . .

We strode along the tracks talking about Verne, about what we wanted to do and had done, whatever came to mind. It struck me how calm I was in spirit. It was hard to believe that I, Randy Bullock, was now walking down a railroad track spotting rabbits and talking about life to some strange straight guy. I, Randy Bullock, who'd had to have something exciting to do every minute in New York or it wasn't right on. Who had to be chasing girls, tripping, or screaming down the streets on a souped-up bike.

Looking ahead at the tracks disappearing toward the horizon, I had an immense, lonely feeling for all the people who had ever walked those tracks with no real motive power in their lives.

By the time we got back to the ranch, Dave and I were good friends. "I understand why you want to go back to New

IT'S GOOD TO KNOW

York, Randy," he said. "You'll find God there, too, now. So it won't be too bad. When you finish there, why not come out to Los Angeles and stay at Renewal House? You can have a room."

"I'd like to, Dave," I answered. "I'll be going home, to Colorado, first. Then, after a while, who knows?" I had to take this one step at a time, but it was a great feeling knowing someone cared enough to offer me fellowship. I knew that I needed to be with Christians, as I came back from that Eye of Japetas.

The next morning, as I waved goodbye to Verne and some of the others at the airport, I hoped Dave was right about finding God in New York, too.

When we landed, it was hot and humid, and New York was suddenly alien and frightening. I figured the best way to lick it was to move fast and get out. I took a subway to my apartment and climbed the stairs, perspiring. Anxiety rose up in me at the sight of a note on my door. But when I read it, my jaw dropped open, and I staggered back. A guy named Spence, a fellow waiter at the Beef and Brew, wanted to buy my damaged Triumph as is for $550. I couldn't believe it! When I came out of orbit, I said, "Thanks, Lord. You made it ahead of me."

By one of these odd coincidences, that I was coming to see weren't coincidences, the amount offered paid off almost to the penny what I still owed Master Charge, a week's rent at Joe's Roach Rest, and a plane ticket to Denver. I had just enough left over for a few phone calls and fares, and used the money the next day wrapping things up, zipping around town saying goodbyes, collecting addresses and gathering my belongings.

Then I called Brian Hurst. He invited me over.

"I'm leaving town, Brian," I said when I'd settled on one of his luxurious couches. "Thanks for trying to help me. I was slightly deranged, to put it mildly."

"When you left here with Lucky to rent that place of

Joe's," he said, shaking his head, "I didn't think you cared whether you lived or died. But, now you pop in looking like a new man."

"I am. I'm flat broke, but I don't owe bread to anyone in this town. No one!"

I said goodbye to Brian, and now I had an airplane ticket, packed bags at a central location, but no money, no way to get them. "Now what, Lord?" I asked. "Are you still there?" I hadn't wanted to tell Brian I was so broke I couldn't even afford carfare. After all, I was supposed to put such things in the Lord's hands. I felt his leading, heard Him saying, "Trust . . . trust . . . trust."

I hurried to the subway. "Look, sir," I said to the token man, "this is the first time in my life I've ever asked for something like this, but I don't have any money and need a token real bad to get downtown, get my bags, and get on a plane to Denver. . ."

He didn't let me finish. He dropped a token in my hand. And then I was on my way home to tell Dad, "I love you." I was so full of love and joy on that plane I just had to turn to the guy sitting next to me and start filling his ear. "I was a plain, everyday, run-of-the-mill freak," I said, "until a few days ago. Now I'm a Jesus freak, I guess." I told him about my weird experiences, then about the three prayers I'd made, two of which had been answered right off the bat. "Now, all I have to do," I concluded, "is tell my dad I love him."

"From what you've told me," the man said in a husky voice, "I'm sure it won't be too late. I . . . I wish my son had had a second chance." He turned away and stared out the window. "He was killed in Vietnam."

Suddenly, I saw the other side! Don Williams' talk on unconditional love flashed, and I saw with my heart what he'd meant. My dad had loved me no matter what I'd done.

By the time the plane landed, I was all together, calm, and at peace with myself.

IT'S GOOD TO KNOW

Ed Kane picked me up at the airport. I stood there grinning at him for a minute, thinking about how we'd gone off so cocky to the big city, how I'd crashed, how he'd seen the light so much sooner.

When I got home, Mom was there waiting to embrace me. "Oh, Randy, you look so thin!"

"I haven't been around your cooking for quite a while," I replied.

That was a signal for Mom to start things happening in the kitchen while we waited for Dad to get home from the shop. I looked over my old room. All my pictures were still on the wall, souvenir programs of plays I'd been in — all the stuff a kid displays in his own room. I felt as though my whole life was passing in front of me. "Thanks, God," I said, "for giving me another chance. I hope I can make good."

I heard a car drive up, then Dad's voice, "Is he here?" I ran downstairs, "I thought I heard you, Dad!" I cried out. I ran to him and gave him a big bear hug like I did when I was a kid. It surprised both of us, but it was what we needed to bridge that gap in time and space.

It felt so good to be with him again. That scene in Washington, D.C., passed through my mind, that flash of wanting to hold Dad's hand. I reached out now and shook his hand. Suddenly I felt very calm and collected. "I really do appreciate all you've done for me all my life, Dad . . . and Mom, too." I paused, then murmured, "I love you Dad . . . Mom."

Dad swallowed but couldn't say anything. He looked at me, though, with a clear, wide-open, loving gaze and he didn't have to say anything.

The next week showed me what the power of love could do. Dad and Mom and I had many talks, and I felt as if they had accepted me as an adult now. We still didn't see eye to eye on everything. I had so much to learn about being a Christian; I didn't know the first thing about the Bible, and I needed some help. I thought this was something that would just come to me by osmosis, or just wishing it — but now I began to see I was wrong.

As the days went by, I could see that I had a whale of a lot to learn, and needed constant fellowship with Christians to keep from slipping back inch by inch. I was just a baby in Christ! There was a painful burden on me to develop myself beyond mere illusion. I couldn't even explain what had happened to me to my own parents. They tried to understand, but I couldn't get through. The words, the testimony, were halting, clumsy. I couldn't overcome the Tower of Babel effect. . .

Worse, temptation leered at me everywhere. All my old haunts taunted me, luring. I wasn't able to completely eradicate those fears that Peter Frankovich had talked about. I had a recurring dread that some day I would wake up dead. Dead in the spirit, with the lice of lust consuming me.

I wanted to be close to Verne and the other Christian friends in California who knew where it was at. Don Williams ran a kind of half-way house in Los Angeles. I could take Verne's VW that he'd left home and surprise them. . .

15

I WAS BEAT by the time I untangled the knot of freeway interchanges and found the address of Don Williams' Westmoreland House, off Wilshire Boulevard. The place was empty! I went to a drugstore nearby, found a pay phone, and called the Hollywood Presbyterian Church. The Church secretary said Dr. Williams was out of town, would I leave a number.

"I don't have a number," I sighed, hanging up.

Then I phoned a number Dave Anderson had given me. He answered. "Oh, yes. Randy. Praise the Lord! Verne's brother. Are you on long distance?"

"No. I'm in L.A. What gives with Westmoreland House?"

"You're in L.A.? Praise the Lord! I didn't even know you had left New York. Why didn't you call or write?"

"I wanted to surprise everyone."

"Well, I invited you to stay at Renewal House. That invitation's still open. I'll explain about Westmoreland when you get here. Where are you?"

"Where am I? Nowhere, that's where. Actually, I'm on Westmoreland Street, right near the House. . ."

Dave laughed. "Randy, you're about one block away from Renewal House!"

When I got out in front of Renewal House, Dave grabbed

my arm from behind, spun me around, and embraced me, right there on the busy sidewalk. A smile cracked my tense face. Dave's smooth, cheerful, good-looking broad face seemed out of place in this sidewalk crowd of furrow-browed, hard-lined, anxious faces.

At Renewal House, the minute I walked into the hall, looking into a huge living room, I saw teenagers sprawled there who brought back my past, hard. Teenagers near my own age, both guys and gals. Some had ugly needle scars on their thin arms and that strange look on their faces, a mixture of complacent apathy, subdued frenzy, and desperate pleading for something better, a look familiar to me from countless glances in mirrors not so long ago.

Several of them slid off their chairs or uncoiled themselves from the floor and hurried out, like children to a father. "Hi, Dave!" a toad-like guy with long black hair greeted us. "We were waiting for you. We've been having one of those 'discussions about Jesus,' and we got some more questions."

"So, you got us another buddy, huh?" a tall, skinny teenager with brown eyes commented. He looked me up and down, looked at my arms, then said, "What's your bag, man? You a speed freak?"

Dave was surrounded, but he obviously didn't seem to have the feeling I had. I felt crowded in, as I had on the jammed freeway, en route to Renewal House.

He laughed and threw his arms out actually huddling with as many as he could reach. "You shouldn't be questioning so much with Jesus Christ in your hearts. Naw, this one's clean. He doesn't have to kick anything now. He's got Christ." He surveyed the scene, as if taking mental roll call. "I see you're all still here."

"Yeah, like you said, Davey," another replied. "But, man, can't I go out a little while tonight — just for some fresh air?"

Dave shook his head, but the smile never left his face. "If you're restless, go to our little chapel and pray. God can calm you, if you'll just try a little harder to let Him into your heart." He turned to me. "Come on, Rand, we'll get you checked in. You must be tired. I have to be running, I'll turn you over to one of our assistants."

In a cluttered little office off the hall, a red-faced guy in his thirties was poring over some papers. "Sid, this is Randy Bullock. You know, Verne's brother. . ."

"Is Verne staying here? Or where?" I interrupted, after nodding in Sid's direction.

Dave looked at me. "Didn't he write to you? He went up to Seattle to spend the summer with a Christian fellow who runs a carpet business, Ken Berven." He smiled as if to reassure me that Verne was all right.

"Anyway. . ." he turned back to Sid, "process Randy in. I have some people at the Grace Lutheran to see. See you later, Randy. God bless."

I recalled that Dave and the Renewal House were part of the Lutheran Youth Alive Movement.

He patted me on the back and hurried out. Before I left the office, Sid asked me to turn over what little money I had, along with my car keys. In exchange, I signed "The Pledge" and received a long mimeographed list of rules and regulations. Sid smiled. "Sorry, Randy, this may seem unnecessary for you, but we have to help these teenagers help themselves. They want to get clean and walk with the Lord, but they're still weak. We have to set an example."

Having come very close to being permanently hooked on heroin myself, I could see why it wasn't wise to have any money around, and all those who stayed here had to agree to the rules. The main guiding hand here was Jesus' love.

Later, after a meal served cafeteria-style in a large, clean dining room, I sat on my bunk in the dormitory on the second floor. This was definitely not the scene I'd envisioned when I'd started for California. I had expected to be with Verne and have a chance to build a brotherly relationship which, till now, had at best been askew. But Verne was thousands of miles away! The troubled soul had wandered again.

A moody blond kid was sitting on his bunk, hands pressed together. When he finished his prayer, he shuffled up to my bunk. "I hear you're Verne's brother."

I nodded. ".Randy." I put out my hand.

We shook and he said, "I'm Ted Peters. Hey, what did you think of Verne having his guitar ripped off?"

"Huh?"

"Yeah. A junkie named Shoes did it. And after all Verne did for him, taking him under his wing, helping him get cleaned up and straightened out. Gave him a bed and told him about Jesus. He was kind of a personal counselor to him."

"You mean Verne's D-35 Martin, that folk guitar our parents gave him the money for when he lost his in Colorado?" I wondered if Ted knew about the Pillar House bust. I held my breath. Maybe the guitar Ted was talking about was just some cheap practice instrument. . .

Ted shrugged. "I know Verne said it was worth about $600."

I jumped up from the bunk. "Where is this guy Shoes?"

"Search me. He got up before anyone else woke up. Took the guitar and split."

"If I ever lay my hands on him. . ." I was fuming. Verne had had a rough hassle as it was. Even yet he was still troubled in the Spirit. He'd already lost a guitar in that bust back home. Or, at least, as far as I knew, he'd never gotten it back. I hadn't talked to him much, but I knew he valued that Martin I'd seen during Five Days in June, and I knew what heavenly music it made.

Well . . . I said a prayer and fell asleep.

Sunny California! I woke up the next morning thinking about sun. I went to a balcony in back and, sure enough, the sun was out, bright, and the smog was thin. Someone came

IT'S GOOD TO KNOW

up behind me. It was Ted. "It would be a good time to go to the beach."

"You're on. Just show me how to get there."

After breakfast and a rap in the chapel, I put on the five-cent shorts I'd bought in Wichita. Ted got permission to leave and we got the keys to my car, and some money I had from Sid.

Ted directed us up to Santa Monica Boulevard, then out towards the ocean. "That main beach is like Coney Island," he said. "Maybe if you drive a little north. . ."

After half an hour, we spotted a small cove where only two or three people were lying in the sand. I parked on the shoulder and within seconds I'd ripped off my T-shirt and was in the water. In another second, I was out again, shaking. "How come the day's so hot, and the water's so cold?" I shouted to Ted.

I tried it again and got used to it, swam until I was tired, then stretched out and let the sun get to my skin.

We had another fellowship in the chapel in mid-afternoon, and I met Pastor Allan Hanson and his wife, Eunice. Pastor Hanson was the director of Renewal House. I found out that Dave floated between Lutheran Youth Alive headquarters and Renewal House and was always in and out.

He had to take care of street meetings and conferences and many other activities. In fact, although he supposedly had a room at Renewal House, next to the suite shared by the pastor and his wife, he only slept there part of the time.

While I was talking to Pastor Hanson, Sid called, "Phone call, Rand. You can take it downstairs."

Phone? For me? Who'd be calling? No one knew I was here.

It was Don Williams. "Dave told me what happened," he said. "Sorry about that, but we didn't know you were coming. We're making tracks to set up a new Westmoreland House, just one block down from the old one. Reason I called, like to have you come down to the Salt Company and get acquainted. Tonight . . . I'd pick you up but my schedule is uncertain. See you there?"

I had been anxious to see the Salt Company operations, which included the coffee house, the Salt Company General Store, and the Salt Company Art "Factory." The name "Salt" derived from the passage in Matthew 5:13 in which Jesus called his disciples the salt of the earth.

That night I got special permission from Sid to take my car and head for the Salt Company coffee house. All I had to do was get a note signed by someone saying that I was there and what time I left. At the coffee house the kids were, while not necessarily clean-cut, nevertheless "clean." Sheer joy was the dominant expression on their faces as they sat at tables or on cushions on the floor while someone strummed a guitar on a low stage in the middle of the large room.

Coffee, cocoa, coke, and other like beverages were slung by a smiling, busy "waitress" whose white gown flashed red, blue, yellow under the lights. You could hear subdued "Praise the Lords." When the guy with the guitar finished playing, someone came to the mike and said, "Let's all sing!"

There was some hand clapping to a rollicking rhythm and I tried to follow the song. Everyone was smiling. Love seemed to permeate the unsmoky atmosphere and people all around me introduced themselves.

Two shadows came into the room. When they were spotlighted for an instant, they turned out to be Don and Dave. I started to get up from my cushion on the floor, but Don saw me and raised both arms. "There he is, Dave!"

They threaded their way through the crowd and literally lifted me off the floor. "Praise God! Meet Randy Bullock, everyone. Verne's brother!"

I told the gathering everything that had happened between Wichita and Los Angeles via New York, Denver and California.

"Your first job," Don said as the three of us sat back down

IT'S GOOD TO KNOW 151

on my cushion, "is to study the Bible. You can't witness very effectively if you don't know the Word. Even psychologists say we can't think unless we have symbols and concepts to think with. Right?"

Dave said, "Verne's told me several times you have a flair for writing, Randy. You took journalism in high school?" He laughed and turned to Don. "I've got his number already." He turned back to me. "We desperately need someone literate on our newspaper, *Speak Out*. It tells all about Lutheran Youth Alive. I'll come around to your bunk sometime this week, and we'll lay it out for you, what it's all about."

By now, it was time for me to leave — curfew hour. I walked out with Don and Dave, and when I got to the bottom of the steps, Dave took my arm and steered me toward a group of girls talking on the sidewalk. He introduced me around. The only name that registered was Karen Mahoney. "Karen's a friend of Don's secretary, Ginger," Dave said. "So we have to be nice to her." They laughed. I tried to laugh. But my attention was riveted on Karen's face, her eyes. . .

As she moved, a street lamp brought out lights in her curly hair, and her eyes. They were blue. True blue!

I had a sure feeling from those eyes that Karen brimmed with honesty.

"Randy just recently met Christ, girls," Don said. "Pray for him."

"I go to Holly Pres Church," Karen said. "You'll be there Sunday, Randy?"

"If you say so."

I waved goodbye and floated to my car. I was hardly conscious of going back to the Renewal House and going to bed.

The next morning, I called Ed Kane in Colorado. Collect. "Why don't you come and join me? You can drive the Simca out. Verne may pop up at any time for his VW, and I'll be without wheels."

"Okay," Ed said.

We'd been like that for years. Impulsive. Not anchored solidly, one or the other ready to get up and go check out the scene where the other was.

I assumed Ed knew about Renewal House. I'd nicknamed it Withdrawal House, and wished at times I could withdraw, that God would lead me elsewhere. But what kind of work would I find? It cost a bundle to be free in L.A., and I was afraid of being alone.

Here in L.A., without such people as Pastor Hanson, Dave, Don, Karen . . . I caught myself. How did her name get into the hat? But anyway, if Ed came he could help me on this newspaper project. I could share with him this absolutely beautiful Christian feeling that made even the rehabilitation center a place of inner peace.

That afternoon, a new "guest" came in. He was new to me, anyway. He had a crooked smile, a mean look in his eyes. "Well, I'm back for some more of that delicious Jesus stuff!" he said, rubbing his stomach. "You weren't here when I split, were you?"

"No. My name's Randy. . ."

"Far out, man. My name is Shoes."

"Bullock," I added, suddenly giving a mean look myself as the name Shoes lit up red. "So, you're the one who ripped off Verne's guitar. That wasn't very Christian. What gives?"

He sagged. "You got me wrong, pal. Dead wrong. . ."

"You've got a lot of guts to come back. . ."

Shoes didn't seem the kind who could understand. If I hadn't been saved, I would gladly have torn him apart, limb by limb. That guitar was Verne's life.

"Where is it?"

He cleared his throat. "I had to leave it for security. I borrowed $25 off a guy."

I reached into my jeans. "I've got the $25. Let's go get

IT'S GOOD TO KNOW 153

it." It was almost the last of the money I'd borrowed from Dad, just before leaving.

I marched him outside and shoved him in the VW. "Just tell me where."

We went to the first place he mentioned, a long drive toward Watts. He came out of the house. "They say he's gone over to a place on Main Street."

I took him to Main Street. And waited.

He came back out of a cheap flop house. "Over on Figueroa." He hesitated. "He's probably actually split town..."

"Find him!" I shouted, making him jump so his head hit the top of the car.

"Okay, okay. Let's try the Figueroa address." He was really shaking now. In front of another cheap hotel, I parked and he went up the stairs.

I waited. And waited. And waited. Night came. I knew Shoes wouldn't. And then a curious thought came into my head: Maybe the Lord didn't want that guitar found.

Despite my disappointment about the guitar, something brightened me up the next couple of days. Don Williams drove over to the House with Jeff Radford, a guy I remembered from Wichita. "Jeff can stay here, and you two can use my car, if you want to," Don said. "I have to go set up a conference, and I'm taking a plane out. The hitch is, drive me to the airport and then pick me up when I come back. You see, praise the Lord, there's method in my madness!"

We drove him to the airport.

On the way back, Jeff said, "I remember you from Wichita. Hey, Rand, let's surprise Don. He's been wanting to get his car repainted since the Resurrection. I'll take it in, if you'll follow me."

That afternoon, we had the car painted at a quickie place. We couldn't use it for a couple of days, but the love we were able to express was more important.

On Sunday, Jeff and I met Don at the airport, and he

flipped when he saw his car. "What a blessed surprise!" he kept murmuring as we drove back to town.

We pulled up to the Hollywood Presbyterian Church just in time for the service. Afterwards Don came with us to the parking lot. A large group was there. "You people really did a fine job! God love you, and thanks."

Someone wanted to take our pictures in front of the car, I got ready to pose. Then, one of the girls in the group turned around, blue eyes under flippy curls. Karen!

I leaped over to where she was, grabbed her around the waist, and pulled her over to the car.

"I . . . I just wanted someone with me in the picture" I gulped.

Snap!

I wasn't sure if it was the camera. Or my heart.

16

KAREN WIGGLED, as I continued to hold her around the waist. The top of her curly head tickled my chin. "He's already taken the picture," she purred. She slipped out from my embrace and looked up at me, her blue eyes sparkling. "I suppose you're going to ask for another take?"

I whispered to Karen, "I'm new on the West Coast. Why don't you show me where the good beaches are sometime this week?"

Karen stared at me. After a long pause, she said, "I'd love to, Randy." She cocked her head. "How about Saturday? You could pick me up at my apartment?"

"What time?"

"Ten o'clock?"

"Sure. See you then, huh?" I had noticed Don looking at me, and I felt uneasy.

"Well, don't you need my address? Or, have you already gotten it on the sly?"

"Ah — yes, I — I need it," I mumbled as everyone laughed.

It felt good, having someone pay that much attention to me. But I wasn't accustomed to this crowd, yet. I didn't really feel "in." I had a "past." Like an answer to my unpleasant thought, a youth came up to me. "Praise the

Lord, Rand," he said. "I'm Bernard. Why don't you come to our men's fellowship Wednesday night?"

"I sure will" I replied. "Thanks."

I left the group feeling ten feet tall. Jesus Christ was with me. I felt the old sin peeling off layer by layer, and love radiating all around.

My biggest problem was not having much money. I'd saved some of what Dad had let me have when I'd passed through Colorado, but that would go fast even though I was getting free board and room. The main skills I had were drama, where it takes a heck of a lot of luck, training, and getting to know a lot of people before you can start making a living. Christ would really have to put in a leading in this direction if I was ever to make good. And — waiting on tables. What a life that would be to look forward to! Trying to find a job in Los Angeles with skills other than in restaurant work seemed an impossibility.

My biggest immediate desire was to grow with the Lord. I wanted to identify with these cheerful, beautiful people. I needed this group. And the way my heart was tripping and the way Karen had stirred me, from the very first instant I'd seen her, I knew I needed Karen . . . needed her more than anything else in the world. It was really amazing the way I felt about her.

I could tell, despite her apparently light-hearted banter, she had been attracted to me, too.

During the following week, I called her and she invited me to come out to a set where her boss was doing a TV commercial. I had to get special permission to leave Renewal House, but I set it up with Karen for the end of the week and meanwhile had a surprise visit from Dave Anderson, who came to see me about writing something for *Speak Out*. When I complained about feeling restricted by the rules, he smiled. "Just have patience and pray, Randy. Something will turn up for you soon to make things better. You're being tested, brother. You've got to have enough faith and love to

IT'S GOOD TO KNOW

glow with His light, to prove it's true what Christ can do. You just dig into that Bible, Rand." He put his arm around my shoulder.

I felt guilty. Every time I thought about the horrors I'd been through in New York, compared with the wonderful people around me now and these young people at Renewal House bravely fighting odd monkeys and dragons, I thought, how lucky can I be? It's all because of Jesus! Praise His name. I found a verse in Isaiah once that expressed my feelings . . . "For you shall go out in joy, and be led forth in peace; the mountains and the hills before you shall break forth into singing and all the trees of the field shall clap their hands."

Dave took some papers out of his briefcase, some back issues of *Speak Out,* and several sheets of written material, including letters. "Would you study these, Randy? We're in a bad way for the next issue. We need editing, a layout, and a couple of pages of text. Here are some letters from Jesus people in other parts of the country. You can print them, make comments about them, answer them in the paper. Whatever you think."

I got busy and, when lights-out came, I went down to the deserted chapel, turned on the altar lamp, and spread the papers on a nearby table, then got the whole thing set up for typing. The last time I'd done this was working on the riot manual. Now I was writing a type of Jesus manual. Instead of designating sewers where protesters could hide from the cops, I detailed ways of making the straight and narrow a joyous path to paradise.

The setting was perfect . . . the darkened chapel, with a picture of Jesus actually glowing, it seemed, with its own light, the quietness . . . He was there in that chapel with me, helping me all the way. I didn't get to bed until 3 a.m. And Dave was impressed, when he picked up the copy the next day.

The prayer meeting and fellowship Wednesday night kept

me up late, too. The Christ-filled human fellowship added a dimension, and I began to feel I really belonged to the group. When I talked to Karen on the phone the next day, she had to tell me we couldn't make that set visit Friday, after all, but she still wanted to go to the beach Saturday.

Saturday I tooled Verne's red VW toward the La Brea Park district of Los Angeles, to Poinsettia Street, where Karen lived.

And entered heaven itself. Just getting to her pad was an experience. I went through an archway into a courtyard completely taken over by a fantastically huge cherry tree, then up steps.

It was really a high class apartment, dominated by yellow and black, long yellow couch, yellow drapes, low Spanish furniture. ". . . my favorite colors," she said, noticing me looking.

She had a record of piano music playing as she got ready, and the magnificent stereo made thundering keyboard magic. Beethoven.

We left the apartment. When we were a couple of hundred feet from the car, Karen suddenly stopped. I'd been holding her hand and almost pulled her off her feet. "What. . .?"

Karen laughed. "I was so startled. You're . . . you're driving Verne's car."

"Verne? Sure."

"I guess I didn't tell you. Verne and I are dear friends."

We started on our way. "I've known Verne ever since he became a Christian," Karen said. "He'd hitched a ride down from San Francisco. . ."

"On fifteen dollars that I loaned him," I interjected.

"A kid . . . let's see, it was Eddie Weyman, took him over to the Salt Company when they got to L.A. Then Devon. . ."

"Devon Hartman and Verne hitchhiked back to Colorado."

"Yes. Well, I met him at the Salt Company before he and Devon started back. I loved his guitar playing and singing,

IT'S GOOD TO KNOW

and he learned some Christian rock before leaving L.A. He picked it up fast. I was impressed."

I had to interrupt for directions.

"You can stay on Wilshire all the way to the beach," Karen said. "Verne always seemed so mixed up. I thought maybe I could help him find the right road in life," Karen said. "He's always jumping around, from city to city, job to job."

I shrugged. "That's the story of my life, too. From one girl to another. . ." I hit the gas harder.

"The way you said that, 'from girl to girl.' You're so much like Verne in some ways." She laughed. "You probably can't see it. But he's always drifting. You are, too." She started humming, then she looked up at me. "Do you suppose Verne's happy?"

"Quite happy," I said. "Are you?"

"I am . . . now."

Something in my heart kept growing and growing. It had been a. . . a moment. The beach was another. I parked on a hill looking down over a tiny cove, and we made our way to the beach, only 15 feet wide, but ours! We were alone.

Karen was a beautiful jewel in this setting of golden sand and blue water. She was lightly built and so graceful. I wasn't much of a swimmer, but she didn't outdistance me. Mostly, we just lay on the sand and talked.

We were on a crash program to know everything there was to know about each other. I told her about my drugstore job while I was in high school, my waiter jobs, delivering messages for Cosmic Messengers. I told her how interested I was in drama, and how the drama training in New York had fizzled out when I began to fizzle out.

"Maybe it would help you get back into the swing if you came out to some of the sets where we do TV commercials," she suggested. She explained that she was a production assistant for Ross McCanse, an executive producer with Sachs, Finley & Kaye advertising agency, on Wilshire

Boulevard. "The Miracle Mile," she said. "We make miracles . . . the agency, God, and I." She laughed. "I'm God's girl Friday and Ross', too. It's a fun job." She leaned over and tickled me. "But none of the men I meet is as good-looking as a Bullock!" She sat up on the blanket. "Why don't you come out to the set Monday around eleven o'clock?"

"It's a date," I murmured. I was absolutely spellbound by this woman, who was everything I'd ever wanted in a woman and more besides. From the looks of it, everything of which she was a part became a miracle. I was becoming a miracle myself.

I was surprised at how much I missed her only an hour or two after we parted. Me, the guy whose relationships had always been so blase and transitory. I couldn't recall having missed anyone before. Karen, Karen, Karen . . . the name sounded delicious and sweet. The blue of her eyes flashed, a particular blue, a different kind of blue that had life to it, as if a color could live! It was what was behind the blue that gave it animation, sparkle, a dizzying lightheartedness. Karen. . .

The thought of missing her was painful, but before settling down for an afternoon nap, I got on my knees and prayed and thanked God, not only for dredging me up from despair's depths but giving me real life again, and love for others. I was so full of love, I hardly knew how to handle it. I dropped off into a blissful, contented sleep with visions of blue eyes and brown hair.

At a tap on my shoulder, I woke instantly. It was Pastor Hanson.

"I was talking with Dave," he said. "Sorry to wake you up, but it was the only time I could discuss it with you. It doesn't sound like much, but would you consider being our Assistant Director here? We can't pay you much — $30 or $40 a week is all — but you'd only have to put in about 30

IT'S GOOD TO KNOW

hours a week. You'd still get your food free. And you'd get more freedom."

"I've got to be dreaming," I muttered, sitting up. Now I would feel useful, as though I was earning my keep. And have some spending money, too.

"Your most important job will be to see that the residents get to bed on time, that the lights are out. A lot of these kids," Pastor Hanson continued, "wrecked themselves physically when they were on drugs. We're trying to build their health, along with their spiritual life." He looked at his watch, smiled. "I've got to run. Keep praying!"

I got down on my knees again — "Thanks, Lord," I said.

When I phoned to tell Karen the good news, she was happy for me. "But I've got some bad news for you..."

I almost choked as I held onto the phone.

"Calm down, Randy," Karen said, laughing. "It's just that we have to postpone that visit to the set once again. You were to come out tomorrow — remember?"

"I'm disappointed, too," I said. "Oh, well... I guess the Lord wants us to be patient."

"But I'll take you to dinner tomorrow night," Karen said. "And before you start objecting, I'll just say, 'objection overruled.' I owe it to you. For letting you down."

I had just said goodbye, when Ed showed up at Renewal House. After some vigorous back slapping, we got down to serious rapping and sharing experiences that lasted off and on until well after lights out. When I got to bed, finally, I was emotionally drained. So much had happened!

Dinner the next evening with Karen was another high point. Mostly, I just feasted my eyes on her. In the semi-dark of a nice restaurant, she seemed to fit in beautifully. Instead of sitting across the table from each other, we sat side by side, and I kept finding my hands straying to touch her hand or her arm, to make contact with her.

She belonged with the sparkle, the glow and the quiet politeness of the classy restaurant, the gleam of fine silver and the flickering of candles. And I belonged with her, with Karen. Karen of the candlelight and Karen of the sunshine. A girl for all seasons.

We sat beside each other in the darkness long after we'd finished eating, holding hands, not wanting to break away. I thought of all the nights I'd wasted in my life, and all the nights of loneliness. "I don't know what you see in me," I said at one point. "But I'm glad you do."

"I like being with you, Randy," Karen replied. "Don't ask me why. You make me feel fulfilled in some mysterious way."

That was how she made me feel! It was really strange, that we made each other feel the same way, used the same terms, as though we were on the same channel.

I kept telling myself in the following days, not to get too excited. What if Karen didn't share my feelings? I prayed about this and felt almost on the verge of tears. I had to fight to keep myself from telling God what to do, wanting to say, "God, make Karen love me." I ended up saying, "Thy will be done!"

The next Sunday, after services, we took a drive through Hollywood. We parked in the Hollywood Hills and looked down at "Tinsel Town."

She had let me drive her little Fiat 850, and I was feeling bigger and better than I had in a long time. I felt full of goodness and love. Big enough and good enough suddenly to put my arm around her, draw her even closer, and kiss her.

She drew back and looked at me questioningly.

"I love you," I explained boldly. Just like that. "I love you, I love you, I love you!" I had said it, and it was said. I thought she might tell me she didn't want to see me again. I was afraid, bold, confident, miserable.

She seemed to freeze for a moment, as though I had not

waited long enough. Then she curled her arm around my neck impulsively and pulled my head down for another kiss. "I love you, Randy," she whispered.

For the next few months, I never did quite come down to earth. I was weightless, totally in love with the kindest, sweetest, most gracious woman I'd ever known. She was a girl who made me feel like a man and restored my confidence. Now only the present moment was important to me, and the two of us together. Nothing could spoil it. I wouldn't let anything ruin it.

One day, wanting to share my joy, I called Verne in Seattle. He was surprised I was in Los Angeles and sounded excited that we'd have a chance to see each other soon, when he came down for a Lutheran Youth Alive Conference in San Diego at the end of August, 1971. Then I told him how I felt about Karen.

He hesitated, then said, "You reckon it's for real this time?"

I laughed happily. "You'd better believe it!"

"Well, if you two feel that way about each other, all I can say is, congratulations! As for me," he continued, "I'm still hurting over losing my guitar. Have to pluck on one you couldn't even give to a pawn shop. I'm still trying to figure out how to get hold of a good one again. But I'll be down to San Diego and see you there. Give Karen my love."

"Sure will." I hung up wondering for a moment how he really felt about Karen.

I thought about what he said about the guitar. I enlisted Dave Anderson and Bob Marlowe, a guy in our group who knew a lot about guitars. We decided to make tracks and surprise Verne when he made the scene in San Diego.

Meanwhile, I continued to "grow" under the tender loving kindness Karen sprinkled on me so liberally, and which I tried in every way to return.

One of the ways she helped me was to make me feel important when we were with other people. Now that I had more freedom, I was able to go with her places where TV commecials were being made. Then, partly with the help of Karen's contacts in both the Christian movement and the motion picture industry, I was chosen to play a small part in a short documentary film for World Wide Pictures.

The film was entitled *Isn't It Good To Know,** and six people from different backgrounds discussed their experiences before the camera. I represented the dope and political radical problem; one girl had been involved in witchcraft and appeared in the film with her husband; another girl had come out of the dregs of society. And there was a straight kid who had simply met the Lord through Billy Graham.

Having a chance to appear in a film, and working on *Speak Out*, I felt as though I was witnessing as well as making progress in my own personal growth. And it was Karen who gave it all meaning. She also helped me regain my lost poise in public. She taught me a lot about food, style, manners, social grace, and appreciating nice surroundings.

Karen and I did a lot of things with our Christian friends, such as Ginger Ellis, Don's secretary, and her boyfriend, Tom. We went to movies together, to Bible studies, to picnics. Both Karen and Ginger were livewires in the Lord, and I was getting with it in a big way myself, learning how to find joy in clean ways, with Christ always one of the guests, a laughing Jesus full of mirth and love.

But the most cherished moments were when we were alone. Karen and I were content to be by ourselves. Nights, after I'd "put the kids to bed" at the House, I'd sneak over to her place, and we would sit up and talk and listen to Beethoven and Chopin on the stereo and just think good thoughts until 2 a.m. I didn't want to leave even then.

We would always be looking for something to do for each other. I was handicapped by not having much money, as I

---
*Not released by World-Wide Pictures until more than a year after the release of *Time To Run*.

IT'S GOOD TO KNOW

waited like all stars have had to do for the big break, and waited on the Lord. So she would insist on paying for a lot of things, even sometimes buying me clothes. She cut my hair, and this was a precious time, when her sweet tender hands would be around my face, my head, her own face near, her humming and talking so close to my ears. I'd grab her and kiss her and sometimes nearly get my ear cut off.

I worked on her car and helped her in other ways, such as moving a piano up to her apartment after she'd decided she wanted to take piano lessons. Yes, Karen and my love for her gave me a new zest for living! God was so good to me, it was hard for me to find ways to thank Him enough.

Our most cherished time of all was when we'd sit on the black-and-yellow couch in her apartment in the afternoon. Every afternoon at the same time, thousands of birds would come to the huge tree that filled the courtyard outside her window. The birds would flutter there and start singing and Karen and I would sit together quietly and never say a thing. We were in each other's arms, calm, completely in love, and totally lost in each other. We were like the wind, in tune with the universe.

Birds seemed to have this harmony. Migrating birds do not seem to need to make audible noises or even visual signals when a change in course is imminent. Suddenly, a whole flock will wheel to starboard all at once. Karen and I were like that, anticipating each other's thoughts, words, feelings. The calmness we felt when we were together was that of feeling perfectly secure, knowing we needn't fear the other's spite or wrath, nor be concerned that the other was playing games.

Our love seemed linked to nature in so many ways — the sun shining through droplets of water to create the colors that brightened our lives, God's pure light spread out. The colors vibrated with sound, too — our voices mingling, harmonizing, laughter trilling at little jokes, serious tones like the bass part of the piano, the melody of our love . . .

rainbow bands like keys on the piano creating this spectrum of loving that lingered in our looks, echoing even after the sound had ceased.

Nature seemed to be ours. We were the sun and the moon and all things in time...

It was almost August, 1971, and I had been working on a surprise for Verne — a way to share this miracle of love that had lifted me out of the depths and into heaven.

17

DAVE ANDERSON AND I had been working for some time on a plan to buy Verne a new guitar at least as good as the wonderful Martin that had been ripped off. To all of the friends I'd made so far, and to all the people I met whom I thought might be sympathetic, I told the story about Shoes and his rip-off deal. "Frankly, I'm broke," I'd tell them. "But if you can spare a buck two-eighty, or whatever, I'm sure Verne and the Lord will appreciate it."

I spent many hours praying during July and August. As soon as I started getting some of the needed money, I went to Bob Marlowe, the leader of the Salt Company music group and one of the finest Christians I'd ever met. He wrote tremendous Christian music, and I thought it would be a tribute to Verne if he had a hand in selecting a guitar to make up for the troubles Verne had been having.

Bob and I went to musical stores and tried out several guitars. After a few weeks, we found one that Bob thought would be perfect for Verne. It had a heavenly sound, and Bob was enthusiastic, so I put all the money I had collected down on it, and the proprietor agreed to hold it. I also set aside a case monogrammed in leather with Verne's initials and, meanwhile, bought some leather and started making a strap for it. I bought finger picks, guitar polish, and two sets of d'Angelico superlight gauge strings that sounded like angels when plucked.

I started getting frantic as August neared an end, and I was still a hundred dollars short of the amount needed to claim the guitar. I gave it to God in prayer, and on the very day of the Congress, the last dollar came in. I paid for the guitar and went to San Diego, to give it to him.

I was backstage putting the strings on and trying to tune it. I said, "Lord, I've never been able to tune a guitar, but if You'll help me, I'll get it tuned enough to give him some idea of how beautiful it sounds." When I finished, I put the guitar in a pre-arranged place near the curtain and waited in the wings until the Christian Jordanaires group completed their song.

Dave Anderson walked out on stage. "I have a special announcement before the next part of the program," he said. "Randy Bullock has a few words for you."

A spotlight followed me, as I joined him, and took the mike. The spotlight was in my face so I couldn't see Verne. I told a story about a guitarist who got a little lonely and began worshipping the guitar. The instrument made him a smashing success, a great singer, and an immensely popular performer.

I kept fun and good humor in my voice as I continued, "But maybe this guitarist worshipped his guitar more than he did God. God chose to take the guitar away from him. The musician repented and learned his mistake, so God decided to reward this singer with another heavenly instrument. Well," I concluded, "God has an award for one of the singers in this audience today — my beloved brother, Verne Bullock!"

"Please come up on the stage to receive your reward, Verne," I said.

Verne shakily made his way up the steps, onto the stage, and to the mike. Both Verne and I were crying, and everyone was applauding wildly. I handed him the guitar and made a little bow, then went down to the audience.

Verne looked it all over, guitar, strap, case. He put the strap around his shoulder, turned away from the mike again as emotion overcame him, and then strummed on it a little. Now facing the audience again, his eyebrows lifted as a smile flitted across his face and he strummed it some more. Then he chuckled, then started to laugh, then looked down at me in the first row. He didn't have to say anything for me to know that guitar was in perfect tune! He didn't have to touch a peg!

The next day, Karen and I took in the remaining events of the Congress. At a music session, Pam Mebane of the Salt Company sang, "High on the Love of My Jesus." And Verne sang, "There are Times When You're Feeling Lonely," and I thought, "Amen, amen!" and hoped those times were past for all of us.

Among the speakers who really got to me was Tom Skinner, founder of Tom Skinner Associates, a team of black men bringing Christ into lives in a radical way. Tom was converted to Jesus Christ while a gang leader in Harlem and had written three books. He had led thousands of people to Christ during his travels across the U.S. and into many foreign countries. What really got to me was his topic — "Radicals for Christ."

To be a radical for Christ, he said, we needed to be not just learned in the Word, but to live the Word, and find our identity as God's children, *in* Christ. It hit hard when he compared the fist-waving radicalism of Barabbas, and the quiet, loving radicalism of Jesus. Barabbas and Jesus both diagnosed the problem the same; only the treatment was different. Barabbas thought he could change the system; Jesus, people's hearts. "If you change people's hearts," He might have said, "the system will self-destruct."

A memorable moment during the Congress weekend was when Ed and I went to our room in the Grant Hotel. While we were out on the balcony of the sixth floor looking down into a park, we saw a group of Christians who'd spilled out onto the streets to testify. There were actually two groups in that park, both armed with guitars. Each formed a circle, and they were close enough so that, from the distance, it almost seemed they formed a figure 8.

One of those circles was composed of kids protesting the war, and they were singing, "One, two, three, four/What are we fighting for?/Don't ask me because I don't give a damn!" The other circle was singing "Thy Loving Kindness" and "We Are One in the Spirit."

Suddenly, before our very eyes, the two circles seemed to merge, and from the park there was a resounding "Praise the Lord!" as though Jesus had, through love, conquered Barabbas. The whole experience of San Diego stirred tremendous emotion. I didn't know how to channel it. I was too new in the Lord!

After returning from the San Diego Congress, I was given a "pass" to attend a beautiful retreat in the San Bernardino Mountains east of Los Angeles. The Hollywood Presbyterian Church group wanted, in exchange for my "free passage," my testimony!

Afterwards, I wasn't sure whether I had said anything meaningful to anyone. However, I did meet a young filmmaker, Robbie Tregenza, who came up to me and congratulated me on my testimony.

I was anxious to get back to Los Angeles and specifically to Karen. For a few weeks Karen and I had each other to ourselves again more often, and somehow we slipped into November. The new Westmoreland House opened, and Ed, Dave Anderson, Don Williams, two or three others, and I moved in. Verne finally made it back and also claimed a bed. As Thanksgiving of 1971 neared, it looked as though we were having a harvest of happiness.

I ached, now, to have a wife, a home, kids. Suddenly, this

was the only important thing in the world. "We are in love, aren't we?" I asked one night in her apartment. "I mean, that leads to . . . Karen . . . will you marry me?"

Karen looked at me for a long time without speaking. Finally, she answered, "We love each other. And I think God loves us. Randy . . . I've been thinking about the same thing, and I knew that one day you'd ask me."

"Well?"

"I want to do what the Lord wants, Randy. Let's pray. Let's see if we can get God's guidance on our plans."

We were silent for several minutes as we concentrated our whole beings in prayer. I wanted Karen so much. I worshipped her. The more I thought about it, the more I was determined that if she would only say "Yes," God would bless our lives for the rest of time and not even death could part us.

Finally, Karen sighed and opened her eyes. "Randy, I keep getting the message that we're to look in the Bible for our answer."

I smiled. I was utterly confident what the answer would be. We were natural for each other and a perfect match. Every time I thought about us, I came up with the same answer. She was the only woman I'd ever known who seemed totally content just to be with me and me alone, and I felt exactly the same way about her.

Could anything be too perfect?

18

I FELT ALL SHIVERY being there alone with Karen and praying about getting married. I was burning with suspense. "Everything in the verses we've been reading looks affirmative to me, honey," I said.

"But, Randy. . ."

"Just listen, honey, Romans 13:10-11 — 'Love worketh no ill to his neighbor: love therefore is the fulfillment of the law. And this, knowing the season, that already it is time for you to awake out of sleep: for now is salvation nearer than when we first believed.' " I looked up from the Bible and smiled. "This is the season, all right! And, notice John 15:12 — 'This is my commandment, that ye love one another even as I have loved you.' "

"We do that, Randy," Karen said, her eyes moist with emotion. Then she looked puzzled. "You can't be so sure from just those words on love and marriage, Randy. If you want something to happen so badly, you might read a meaning into it that isn't really there."

My heart was on the off-beat. I wanted marriage for us so badly. There was an awful undercurrent of wondering if Karen was trying to find excuses. "Hey, you're not dubious, are you?" She'd just read a passage about grass withering and flowers fading.

"Don't you think that's something to think about?" She went on quickly, then she smiled and took my hand. "That might have something to do with our difference in age, Randy. Have you thought about that?" She made a gesture with her other hand toward her hair. "Seven years older . . . my hair will be grey first. I don't want you to feel I'm too far ahead of you, growing old while you're still young."

I laughed. "Karen, Karen . . . our time is now! You and I are both ageless and timeless because we're in love. We're outside of time and space. Two people in love are in a separate reality. There is no time and space."

I don't really remember what happened then. Karen kind of nuzzled up to me, then gave a big sigh. "I just hope this is what God wants. I know I want it like crazy! Ohhhh, Randy! Let's do it!"

"Oh, wow! When?"

I was trying for the next few minutes to come down from space. So short a time, yet look what had happened! We sat there by the window looking out into the courtyard and, even though it was night, in our imagination we talked to those thousands of birds that sang our love song on sunny afternoons.

The next few weeks we talked about wedding plans, which had evolved to a "city" wedding in L.A. and a "mountain" wedding in Colorado, so her family and the Holly Pres Church could resound with the happy bells, as well as the vast mountain land of Colorado.

I knew I had to accumulate some money, so I got a job waiting tables at the Boston Half-Shell Restaurant near where Karen lived. I also checked out my chances of enrolling in some school for a course in production and film-making. The past reared its Dracula face. They said, "Clear up that University of Colorado mess and come back."

I wrote to the university to see what I had to do, and they said, "Come back and repeat those courses you freaked out on, man, and we'll give you a groovy record."

Karen said, "Do it."

"You mean you'd be willing to work while I finish school? Subsidize a husband?"

"Sure, why not?" Karen flung back. "Listen, lover, it's an investment in my future, too!"

Karen was easy to lean on, but I wanted to stand on my own, too.

Meanwhile, Verne suddenly reappeared on the scene. I had to restrain myself from telling him how near I was to becoming a married man.

He and Ed came over to Karen's apartment, and we fooled around on the piano and sang crazy songs. Then Verne pulled out one of those perennial pieces of paper he always had wadded in his pocket so carelessly with words and music all over it. "Here's one I did a while ago, Randy. I call it Karen's Song." He sat at the piano and turned to Karen and then started singing along with the melody. It reminded me of Robert Service's "Shooting of Dan McGrew".

> There are times when you're feeling lonely,
> There are times when you're feeling blue,
> And the only one who can satisfy is your lady,
> But she's not with you.
>
> Now I may not have much money
> To buy you diamond rings,
> But what I have, I'll give to you.
> Here's my heart and the songs it sings.
>
> For those times when you're feeling lonely,
> And those times when you're feeling blue,
> Just remember babe, how much I love you,
> And remember, that my love is true.
>
> There are times when you need somebody,
> Just to give you a helping hand,
> And the only one who can satisfy,
> Is your lady 'cause she understands.*

IT'S GOOD TO KNOW

I sat there, dazed by the depth of feeling in the lyrics and the quality of the music. I realized this was just a song and that the singer, a professional from way back, was just doing the usual things good singers do, putting his whole heart and soul into what he was singing. Just as when I got on a stage with a part to play, giving it all I had and making it seem for all the world as though it was the real thing.

I jarred myself out of what was almost despair and, finding myself trembling, jumped to my feet. "Verne! That's really tremendous! You know what you've got there old buddy, don't you? A hit, man. A real hit! Groo-oovy! Isn't it, Karen . . . Karen?" I looked at her, then whirled back to Verne. "See, Karen thinks so, too! She's got tears in her eyes. You'd better promote that one, old buddy."

I just had to give him that credit. And to believe . . . well, to believe that he had sat down to write a good song and had succeeded and should be praised for his efforts.

What else should I have thought? He was my brother.

Christmas was approaching. Verne, who had a room in Westmoreland House down the hall from my room, stopped by one day. "I'm going home."

"Home? You mean, Colorado?"

"Yeah."

"Oh. For Christmas. Well, okay, then. Give Dad and Mom my love and wish them a Merry Christmas for me."

"Sure," Verne said. "But I don't think I'll be coming back."

I stared at him. "But, I thought you and the people here. . ." Then I shrugged, smiled. "Well, okay, then." I laughed. "That's the story of our lives . . . I came out here to be with you, and you weren't even here. Then. . ."

Verne had a funny shaking smile. "Yeah," he said. "Life is . . . the blues."

I was even more surprised when I found out that Ed was going with him and also probably wouldn't return. He was going to resume his studies at Denver University.

Well, they would be with their families. I had a new family, Karen's family, to get acquainted with.

To make up for my not getting to be with my folks in Colorado, I wanted to send some goodies home, but I wasn't making much money, and after paying some back bills, I hardly had enough money even for something for Mom. I knew Dad would understand if I couldn't send him anything.

Because of my impatience and lack of funds, Christmas was not as cheery as it should have been. I tried to summon up the spirit and join in the Christmas carols. By reminding myself it was Christ's birthday I should be celebrating, I managed to achieve a measure of joy. Most of all, being with Karen was happiness.

After the Christmas holidays, I managed to get in some extra hours at work and tuck away a bit of bread. I was impatient to announce our engagement and wedding plans — to know them myself!

My preoccupation with myself was distracted for a little while when I got a chance to do a small part in a film being produced by Robbie Tregenza who'd heard my testimony at Forest Home in the San Bernardino Mountains. He was doing a 16mm, 20-minute documentary on finding Christ. I had to grow a beard . . . and I played the part of an angel.

In January, Karen answered my knock on her door, and I flew in as usual and grabbed her around the waist to dance her to the couch where we sat so often. Then I noticed her eyes were wide and clouded. "What's the matter?"

"Kentucky Fried Chicken. . .," she stammered.

"Karen! After the way you fix chicken, you're not suggesting we settle for something like that?"

She gave kind of a half laugh. "No, no. It's nothing like that. They were our biggest account. Our bread and butter account. They . . . they cancelled."

"Well, it's not the end of the world. You take your boss's business too seriously."

She sighed. "I wish it was just my boss. You don't understand. Ross has already lost a couple of accounts. He was looking for a couple of new ones. He said, 'It looks bad for the television department. I have to let everyone go, Karen!' That's what he said."

We sat on the couch and I squeezed her hand. "There can be a bright side to this, baby," I said, "if you want to look at it. It's our chance. Let's make tracks for Colorado. We can have the best of two worlds."

Over the next few days, the shock of losing a really great, top-paying job wore off and she began to look forward to the change. She sent her recommendations to several places in Boulder and Denver to try to set up a job while I sent my enrollment forms to the University of Colorado.

"Let's make tracks, sweetheart," I said one day in February. I suddenly realized we had to figure out how to get all her stuff that she didn't sell or that she didn't want to sell from Los Angeles to Denver. I decided there was a way to mix pleasure with business. I called Doug Stiverson. "You got any vacation time coming?" I asked.

"Sure, why?"

"Well, why don't you come out to L.A., meet my fiancee, Karen, see the sights, and then help us drive all her stuff and my backpack to Boulder?"

"Sure," Doug replied.

When Doug showed up, I felt I had to be his host and show him the City of the Angels. He livened up the scene and we were just like kids again. He and Karen hit it off, but one thing she couldn't quite get straight — how we could enjoy spending so much time seeing the town on rented motorcycles.

It felt like old times being in control of a bike, and I was so caught up in it that the money I'd saved for our trip back to

Colorado smoked away out of the exhaust pipe without my realizing what was happening.

After most of my money was gone, I came to. And then turned to Karen and asked, "Well, are you ready? What are we waiting for?"

Karen looked at me as though I was off my rocker. "I haven't been able to say two words to you all week. Now that I've got you cornered again, I'll say three — I love you. How's that?"

It was nice. I'd been neglecting her too much.

But then she found out that I'd blown all my money.

"Real great!" she said, sighing, and agreed to lend me the money from her savings.

The next morning, early, with the Simca and the Fiat packed to the top, we took off.

It was late at night when we drove into Denver, after three days on the road. The Fiat had broken down and we left it beside the highway with plans to come back for it later. I was looking forward to surprising Mom and Dad with Karen, as I hadn't said exactly when we would be there. "You just wait and see, honey," I said as we drove into the driveway at last. Karen had been worrying about coming in on them at the late hour, but I knew better. "They're used to all of us doing that." We got out and headed for the front door. "That's funny," I said. "It's only 10:30. They're usually up late." The house was dark, not even a porch light shining.

Wayne answered the door after a series of lights came on throughout the house. "For Christ's sake, Randy!" my brother Wayne hollered. "Why don't you once be considerate enough to let someone know you're coming!"

"Well, uh, er, we had car trouble," I tried to explain. And I knew what would take the sour look off his face. This was hardly the welcome I'd expected. "Where's Mom and Dad?"

"Mom has just had an operation, Randy, and she's flat on her back," Wayne finally said.

IT'S GOOD TO KNOW

Dad came into the room still blinking from the light and tying his robe around him. I jumped up and stuck out my hand. "Randy!" We shook hands, and he looked at Karen. "And this must be the future bride. Welcome to the Bullock's, Karen." Dad sat down on the couch beside us, still kind of half awake. "I'm sorry we weren't up, but I guess Wayne has told you the situation."

Karen and I looked at each other. I wasn't sure what to say, then Wayne came to our rescue. "Look, I was about to suggest that Randy and I sleep downstairs in the rec room, and Karen can have my room. Aren't there some extra mattresses down there, Dad?"

I was relieved. Karen looked tired, and I was exhausted. I hated to think about having to go back for her Fiat tomorrow. Another whole day on the road. What would Karen do while I was gone?

Wayne and I brought some stuff in for Karen and retired to the basement. I kissed her goodnight. "Things will be better tomorrow. After we get the car back we can decide what to do."

"But, Randy," she was crying. "I can't stay here. It's not fair to kick Wayne out of his bed. Didn't you know your mother was going to have this operation?"

"Oh, yeah" . . . I kind of vaguely answered. "Now I remember Dad saying something about it in a letter. But I don't think he said exactly when."

Karen shook her head and shut the door. I could tell she was upset, but I was too. How was I suppose to know the whole place would be in an uproar, just because Mom had gone to the hospital?

Doug came by early the next morning and we borrowed Dad's jeep and headed over the mountain. The Fiat wasn't easy to tow with all the junk inside and the pass was dangerous with rocks falling all over the place. They were threatening to close off the other end. "That's all we'd need," I told Doug.

It was a bad scene at home. Karen crowded into Wayne's room, Wayne upset because he had just lost a good job and a girlfriend, Mom still on her back . . . I was ready to throw it all in and head back to California.

Then I remembered what we had come for. We were starting a new chapter in "The Book of Love," by Randy and Karen.

**Karen Song* by Verne Bullock. ©1970 Uriah Music Company, P.O. Box 342, Elizabeth, CO 80107. All rights reserved.

19

"I'M SORRY you had to bring Karen into all this. She's not seeing us at our best." Mom lay back on the pillows with a sigh. "I hope she'll be happy in Denver, Randy. Don't forget, she's new here, and you aren't."

I hardly heard what Mom said. I was anxious to split. Doug and Ed and I were on our way to the race track, just for a spin around. Karen had gone downtown to look over the shopping area.

I needed to get out. The house was closing in on me. Wayne was crashing around in the basement in one of his moods. I couldn't even talk to him. He didn't make sense. Just kept muttering about love and marriage.

As for myself, I hated the feeling of being 22, and not even quite sure what I was going to do with my life. Cramped up in a small house, dependent on my parents again, having to tell them where I was going, what time I'd return.

Every time I met someone on the street, they'd ask me what I was going to do, what school did I finish, where was I heading. How could I know? All I could do right now was look for a job.

I took Karen to the drive-in one night, but we hardly saw the movie. She was tense. Her eyes were dark.

"What's the matter, honey?" I asked. "Are you homesick already?"

"Homesick, at my age? No, just. . ." She hesitated so long I turned to look at her. "It's your . . . your house. I want out! Oh, Randy, let's find a place for me in the mountains."

"But the mountains cost a lot more to live in . . . more than you can afford right now."

Karen glanced back at the movie. She was silent for quite a few minutes. She had a strange look on her face. Kind of a faraway look. "We aren't going to give up our dream of the mountains, are we?"

"Naw . . . but we've got to wait for the right time, Karen. Why don't you try to find a little apartment right in Denver? Then, when you get a job, you'll be centrally located and. . ."

Karen sighed. "I suppose you're right." She snuggled up close and we watched the rest of the movie.

"Want to have a bite to eat at my old favorite hangout?" I asked her after the movie was over.

"Sure. You know, Randy, we've been here almost three days, and you haven't shown me around . . . like where you went to school, the drugstore you told me about, your 'old hangouts'." She was looking around, as we whizzed by some of them. "Where did your mother say Verne was?"

"I thought she said he was working in some meat-packing plant in Elizabeth . . . yeah, that's where. Look," I pointed out the window, "there's the old alma mater. It looks even bigger now."

Karen glanced over quickly, then back at me. "Elizabeth is in the mountains, isn't it?"

"No, it's just a little farming community. I don't know why he's given up singing. I thought he had it made." I shrugged. "Everybody in my family seems to be having their problems. Except us."

That was the last time we had a chance to go to a movie,

for a while. I got a job where Doug worked, at the Fay Myers Motor Company. I had to leave by 8 a.m. to get there, and it turned out to be a 52-hour-a-week job, selling motorcycle parts. I hardly had a chance to see Karen with my work load.

Doug was racing, too, and his enthusiasm resparked my interest. I had my eye on a Yamaha like his. This was his first season, and he was doing better than when he had his old two-bit bike. I watched him win a race on the following Sunday.

One night after Wayne had gone to sleep, I thought about something Karen had reminded me of. I hadn't prayed much since we'd arrived in Denver. Our whole environment had changed so quickly, I hadn't checked to see whether God was even in Denver.

"Randy, we've got to pull together . . . we need God here, too."

But we were so busy getting settled. Karen had found a job, too. With a film company. And she'd found herself a basement apartment clear across town in a suburb called Bear Valley. It was a nice house, owned by three old ladies. You had to go through the main entry of the house and then down some steps to her place. The furniture was early American and the place was rather cozy.

I moved Karen in one night after work. "Thanks, Rand," she said tiredly as she looked around at the mess.

"Sure you don't want help putting stuff away?" I asked, shifting from one foot to the other. "I'll tell Doug and Ed to wait a little longer."

"No, you go on. I've got to figure out where to put things."

"Okay, hon. I'll give you a call tomorrow night." I gave her a quick kiss, copied down her phone number, and left.

After I got home from work the next evening, there was a letter waiting for me, resting on the table where Mom always used to put my mail. It was from New York. I opened it and forgot all about calling Karen. The letter was from the attorney who had handled my crash on the Cosmic bike. The suit was finally settled . . . for over a thousand! I gave a loud whoop and ran to the phone to call Doug.

"Better get ready to move over to one side, old friend," I said when Doug answered, "because I'm going to be winning some of those races myself. Want to go downtown and scope out that Yamaha 360 with me?"

When Dad got home, I showed him the letter and told him what I wanted to do.

"Find out how much the bike is Rand, and since we've got the definite word from that attorney, I'll put up the money. You can pay me back when you get the check . . . if it's close to the amount, I mean!" He was laughing at my excitement.

"Don't sweat. The one I have in mind should be right on." I put my hand on his shoulder. "This means I can race, Dad."

I split right after dinner, and Doug and I tooled over to the Yamaha showroom. We looked at the 1972 model 360 and priced it out. "This is right on, pal. Only about $10 difference than what's coming."

I ordered the Yamaha 360.

The next day I kind of floated around the salesroom getting parts and thinking about what Doug and I were going to do to the bike to modify it for racing. We'd have to work every night of the week to get it ready for next Sunday's race, but I was confident we could do it. I kept meaning to call Karen, but somehow I just couldn't stop working on that bike.

By Thursday night I decided I really had better call Karen. The bike was finished.

"Guess what, baby?" I said when she answered.

There was silence on the other end.

"Hey, what gives? I can hear you breathing. You feel like having a visitor tonight? I've got a surprise for you!"

IT'S GOOD TO KNOW

Karen liked surprises. "I'll be here. It better be good." She hung up.

The weather had turned warmer, and it was a beautiful Spring evening, but Karen's tone had sent chills down my back.

I jeeped across town and coasted in quietly, parking the Jeep on the sidewalk. Karen met me there and guided me down the steps to her apartment without talking. She acted funny.

Coming up behind her, I ruffled her curly hair. "Come on, baby. You haven't even given me a kiss."

"Well, what do you expect?" she said, turning around and glaring at me. "You move me into this basement apartment, where half the things don't work, don't call me for four days, and then expect me to be all excited and surprised about a new motorcycle you've bought and worked on every night this week."

"But I've been working . . . and getting the bike ready." I sprawled on the couch and reached out to pull her down beside me. "What's really bothering you, Karen? This isn't like you." I put my arm around her and made her relax against my shoulder.

"It's just . . . well . . . Rand, you've seen your friends more than you have me! It used to be just us, now it's Doug, racing, Ed, your folks, — and then me!"

"Karen, you're the only person who really matters to me. It is nice to be back with my old friends, but I didn't realize you felt left out. I guess when I've been out with them I've just let the clock slip back and have fallen into my old 'carefree' habits. I won't let it happen again, honey."

Karen didn't say much. I stayed long enough to tease her out of her mood, but I wasn't quite sure if we had patched up our thing.

Our time in space just stood still for a while. I called her more often after that, and we talked about our jobs, and I tried to tell her more about the races coming up. She begged off from the first one, saying she didn't want to distract me, and wanted to catch up on things from the move.

After a couple of weeks, our friendship helped us to work our way back to the same relationship we'd had in L.A.

I wondered why, whenever Verne was in town, we didn't get together. Karen said she'd talked to him on the street a couple of times; I hadn't even known he was in town.

Karen finally saw how keen I was on racing. "You have to have five first place finishes or seven second place ones in the racing season to get in the big time, honey," I told her on the phone one night. "You get money . . . not just trophies. Doug is already up in the big leagues. I've got to catch up!"

Every spare minute I had, I rode. Doug encouraged me, and so did Dad. I took Karen to the weekend races, but hardly saw her during the week. Racing made her very nervous. 'I'll try not to worry about you. I don't want you mutiliated!"

The next day at work a call came over the loudspeaker. "Randy Bullock, long distance, line 6."

It was Kenette Riggs and Robbie Tregenza with World Wide Pictures in California.

"Look," Robbie said, "we're making this movie, *Time To Run,* and we need a preacher. No one fills the bill here. I showed them the footage you did for me, and they liked it." He paused a minute. "You still there?"

"You better believe it!"

"They want to know if you can fly out to L.A. and do the part. Can you get any time off there?"

I gulped. For something like that, I'd quit! "Yeah, sure. No sweat. When?"

"About the last of April. We'll send you a script and all the details. How's Karen?"

"Ohhhh, great. Just great. Thanks for the break. I'll be there. Just send me the word." I hung up and whirled back to the counter, trying to come down to earth.

All kinds of wonderful thoughts were going through my mind. I could hardly wait to get to the phone to call Karen, but that was taboo on her job.

Doug kidded me the rest of the day about "Randal the Great" making good at last in the movies. Or he'd come over and take a part out of my hand and bow . . . "Allow me, Mr. Bullock, the *star* shouldn't get his hands dirty."

That evening, I went over to see Karen. "I had a long distance call from Robbie at work."

"Not Robbie Tregenza, the one who had you do that short film?"

"Karen, you're marvelous. How could you remember all those people? We've been away from them since January."

Her face lit up. "Was he trying to find Verne?"

"No! Me!" I hugged her tightly. "They want me for a part in a movie they're making for World Wide . . . *Time To Run,* and it'll be sometime in April. Also stars Randy Carver and Barbara Sigel. Honey, why don't you plan on coming with me? We could see all our old friends . . . you could see your mother."

"Oh, Randy!" she cried. "You must be nuts. I can't leave this job just any old time."

"I guess I didn't think," I said dejectedly.

"It'll be a good opportunity for you to have some Christian fellowship, and you can see Don Williams, too."

"Say, maybe this is a good omen. A new opportunity."

"What about school, Randy?"

"I don't know. I'm sure this won't take too long. Say, speaking of school, are we going to look for a place in Boulder when I get back?"

"One thing at a time!" She put her hands on her hips and surveyed the room. It had some new touches, I noticed. "Randy, I don't know if I can move again right away . . . my job . . . well, I guess we can leave that discussion for a while, yet."

I hadn't said anything to my boss at the shop about the call from World Wide, and it was a good thing. They had to postpone it three times! I didn't want him to get the idea I might be a bit flaky about this job. I needed it to keep raking in the dough for racing.

Mom was beginning to be up and around more. One morning she sat down at the table with me. "Randy? Have you seen Verne since you got back?"

"No, I always seem to be gone. Why?"

"The last time he was here he just didn't seem very happy. I thought . . . maybe you might know why." She looked thoughtful. "He was so different . . . kind of deranged almost. Kept saying he just wanted to be left alone and not to 'bug him'. I couldn't ask him any more questions. . ."

I shook my head. "I guess it's something he'll have to work out himself." I got up and put my chair back. "Look, I gotta split, or I'll be late for work. I'll think about it. Don't overdo now." I gave her a quick hug and flew out the door.

I finally heard from World Wide and began to make plans for the trip. I had memorized my lines and felt confident about the whole thing. Verne and his problem kept flitting through my mind, but I didn't have any time to do anything about it. I didn't have any answers, either.

I bought a brown striped polo shirt and some new boots. The script called for casual clothes. I had plenty of jeans but I thought that polo shirt would give just the right touch.

Karen liked it, too. We spent Sunday together, trying to make up for some of the time we wouldn't see each other. The room came alive with Karen's beauty when she served dinner by candlelight. .She had on a flowery peasant-like long dress, and it made me just want to touch her all through dinner.

After dinner we were feeling especially romantic and we left the dishes for once. Karen put a stack of records on the stereo and we gravitated toward the couch.

The music, one of Chopin's nocturnes, put us in a dreamy

mood, and I was never more completely sure that she was all I wanted in life. I whispered, "That nocturne is the moon and the stars and you all rolled into one, honey . . . starlight." I paused. "Even, heartbreak." I laughed. "How come it never sounded like this before?"

The next few days on the job were a drag. I just put in my time and forced myself to stay on the track. I didn't want to goof myself up for coming back to this job.

Thursday evening, Karen called. My heart was pounding when she asked me to come over. "She must feel like I do," I said to myself as I drove over to her place. I felt strangely calm and happy.

The minute I walked down the stairs and into her apartment I wanted to take her in my arms. She had on long pants and my favorite shirt, a blue, long-sleeved cotton one with little cloud-like pastoral scenes all over it.

"Why don't you sit in the rocking chair?" She pulled her chair over closer to mine as I sat down, and then she put her hand on my knee. It was then that I realized that we hadn't even kissed "hello". I leaned over and kissed her.

"Randy . . . there's something I have to tell you."

"Yeah?"

Her voice sounded strange. I smiled into Karen's blue eyes. Then I saw that they were troubled.

"What's the matter, hon?"

"Randy . . . it's . . . it's Verne. I, we. . ."

I leaned forward. "Is he hurt or something?" I felt guilty for not checking on him when Mom had suggested.

"No, he's not hurt. At least not now. But he was. Ever since you told him you loved me, Randy," she went on with a rush. "Try to listen closely and try to understand. This isn't going to be easy."

Suddenly, I didn't want to hear what Karen had to say. I didn't want to "listen," and I didn't want to "understand."

"Verne came into town yesterday and called me," she went on. "Before I was even out of bed. He said he had to see me . . . right away. It was a matter of life and death." She looked at me pleadingly. "He sounded desperate, Randy. So I told him to come on over."

"What did he say?"

"He said he loved me, and he wanted to marry me. Right away! He even had it all set up."

"He *what!*"

I leaned back in the chair and laughed. "Mom must be right, she said he was acting kind of crazy. . ."

But Karen didn't let me finish, just blurted out, "I found out I love him, too, Randy. And we're going to be married this week. This Sunday to be exact, at 12 noon in a little mountain church called Rockland Community. We prayed and prayed about it, Randy, and we're sure it's God will."

"God's will!" I choked out. "But our marriage was supposed to be. . ." I couldn't say anymore. I just sat there, stunned.

I looked around the room. Almost five minutes went by before I could say anything. Some music was on the stereo, but I didn't even recognize what it was. I looked at Karen and around the room.

Now I wanted to reach out and touch her, but I couldn't. She belonged to someone else now. She belonged to my brother, the very person who got me to know the Lord, got me out of New York, brought me back to *life*, so I could meet the only other person I had dearly loved. Karen!

I finally looked over at her and murmured. "Well, best of luck. Congratulations!"

"Will you come to the wedding?"

A cold shiver went down my spine. "No, Karen. I can't. You know I can't go, don't you?"

I wanted to put my head on her shoulder and pull her close to me, as I had on so many occasions. For the first time

IT'S GOOD TO KNOW

in our relationship, we weren't lost in love. I couldn't even rely on being a friend right now. I started to cry.

When I got control of myself, I tried to put her mind at ease. I could see pain on her face, too. "I'm going to try not to think about this until the movie is completely finished. I'll do my best. My plane leaves for L.A. on Sunday morning at 11:30." Tears were welling up again, and I knew I had to get out of there fast! When I got up my legs felt like rubber.

"If this is what you and Verne want, Karen, then so be it. I wouldn't want everyone to see me crying. Weddings are supposed to be happy occasions!"

I had reached the door and turned and headed up the stairs, stumbling on the last three.

20

ON THE WAY HOME I knew how someone must feel with all the blood pumped out of them. Or how a shadow feels. I didn't say anything to my parents. Surely, they must know. Why didn't they bring the subject up? Explain to me, if that was possible? But they acted as if nothing had happened. I thought it was up to them to say something first.

I went to bed, but I couldn't sleep, yet couldn't get up either. I was in shock, not yet feeling the full force of the pain.

For the Memorial Day races at the end of the month I needed every penny I could lay my hands on, otherwise, I wouldn't have planned to go to work the next two days, Friday and Saturday. I kept trying to think of bikes as I lay on my bed, feeling as though ropes were binding me and feeling every knot. Man, I'd show them in the races!

Friday was a long, hot, noisy day. The worst part of it was seeing constant reminders of romance, even there in the bike shop, as bikies came in with their girlfriends, joked and flirted with each other while they waited for parts. Everything reminded me of . . . of what I wanted to forget.

The day finally dragged to an end. Usually, on Friday night, I'd have called Karen, and we would have gone out

IT'S GOOD TO KNOW

somewhere. Now I couldn't. I went home, feeling pain inside as though something had been ripped out of my body.

When sleep finally came, it was no escape. Night jeered me with a thousand voices. "Sucker! Sucker! Sucker!" Night seemed to taunt. I kept dreaming about Karen blowing a kiss to Verne behind my back . . . meeting him in secret places. They'd just been using me. I was convenient. Sordid scenes flashed, and then the scene of that Thursday evening when Karen told me the news.

Next night I was packed, ready for the trip to California. I felt completely miserable. I went out and walked around town for a little while, wanting to be alone. When things were heavy, this was my way. I stopped at a pay phone to call Ed and ask him if he'd drive me to the airport in the morning.

I walked around some more, but the tenseness and the misery wouldn't leave me. I saw a kid on the street who was a pusher. I stopped him. "Oh, Randy. Hi," he said. He kind of laughed. "How's the Jesus freak these days?"

"I'm just a freak, pal. . ."

In the morning, I waited for Ed out on the front porch. I hadn't said anything to my family — no goodbyes.

"I can tell something's wrong," Ed said after we'd driven for a couple of minutes.

"What else is new?" I said. Then I told him what happened.

Ed freaked out. "It's not true!" he screamed. "How could they?"

"They did."

"Oh, those great Christians! How could your own brother do that to you? I hate them both! Nobody could do a thing like that!" Ed was wild. He drove like a maniac, taking it out on other drivers, the car, everything. "I can't understand it. They can't be human. . ."

"Ed! Ed! Drop it!" I yelled. "It's the last thing I want to talk about!"

Shortly, I went aboard the plane — a Continental DC-10, put on my earphones and found myself listening to Beethoven's Pastoral Symphony. Beethoven. . .

Then we flew over the church where Karen and Verne were being married, the little church on the mountain which was to have been the setting. . .

The knowledge of what was happening right now below, combined with the music, tortured me. Tears streamed from my eyes. I wiped at them with a handkerchief, furious that I hadn't been able to keep them locked up deep inside.

During the last few minutes of the flight, I tried to psyche myself into trying to be convincing in pulling off the Jesus stuff for World Wide. After all, I kept telling myself, a job's a job.

I didn't exactly know how to face them. Would they see that something had changed with me? Something was missing? That the brief glow of Jesus was snuffed out?

I wasn't looking around as I walked off that plane. Then, suddenly, I was surrounded. With smiles! My World Wide friends gave me a royal welcome, including Robbie Tregenza, his sister, Rebecca, Mike Hooser, film editor for World Wide and Kenette Riggs, who did the script transcription for the movie. Kenette was married to Bob Riggs, son of Charlie Riggs, Billy Graham's executive assistant.

I hadn't really thought about being met at the airport and was completely caught off base when Robbie Trengenza rushed to me, threw his arms around me, and said, "How's Karen?"

It was as if I'd been shot. I looked him straight in the eye, and said, "An hour and a half ago she married my brother, Verne."

"Come on, tell us the truth."

Robbie stared at me, then finally said, "He means it."

We got in the car to take me to Bob and Kenette Riggs' place, and after several minutes of silence, they started talking about plans for the filming. "Our problem, first,"

IT'S GOOD TO KNOW

Kenette said, "is to decide on the exact location and where the cameras are going to go. We can go out tomorrow afternoon with the director and get our bearings."

I was glad to be staying with Bob and Kenette Riggs. They didn't know Karen, hadn't known about our relationship. It was more comfortable that way.

The next day, in the car, I found myself winding up, up into the Hollywood Hills. I shrugged. Since that plane ride, I'd been building a hard shell around me. Except for a momentary shiver, I didn't feel anything. No woman, no God, no memory, nothing could get to me. I'd made myself impregnable. I was here to do a job, and the Hollywood Hills could just as easily have been the Alps, the Andes, or the Himalayas.

We stopped near Lake Hollywood, and then started walking around, as the director, Jim Collier, and the others staked out the ground where I would be and where 300 long-hairs, playing the part of kids at a rock religious festival, were going to be.

The movie concerned a long-haired, college-age kid, Jeff Cole, who was at odds with his father, over his father's work as a nuclear scientist working for a power company. Jeff worried about pollution. He ran away and failed to get his girlfriend, Michelle, to live with him. Caught, the boy refused to admit to his father he was wrong and ran away again.

Jeff's mother, on advice from Michelle, who had recently found Jesus, sought Jeff at a religious music event. Meanwhile, Jeff was on the loose. He returned to the general area finally, after some rough experiences, and went to a Jesus People rally to seek out Michelle. Michelle tipped off his parents, they found him there, and father and son finally were able to say to each other "I'm sorry." The whole family was drawn closer in the realization that they had left love out of their lives.

I was to play the part of a preacher, when the mother goes

to the park the first time. The director showed me, finally, where they thought I should be for my preaching scene, and then we went back to town.

On Tuesday, I watched them shoot sequences on the set in Burbank. We saw the father at work in the computer section of the nuclear power plant. Jim Collier explained what was going on. A little later, I sat with Randy Stonehill, who had written the music for the scene I was to play, and we dubbed some sound for my scene while the others were cutting and changing around music on a tape for their scene.

The new experiences helped me to forget what had happened. I was in another world and playing a part. I was taking each step one at a time and had told myself over and over, what's done is done. As Shakespeare said, "What's gone and past hope should be past grief."

The next day, Wednesday, we went out to Lake Hollywood, and I stood on the sidelines.

Shots were taken of Jeff's mother coming to the fringes of the park seeking Jeff. She and a friend, Mr. Green, are accosted near the side of a blue bus by a freak. "Where's it happening?" Green asks the freak. "Top of the hill!" the freak replies, handing them some tracts. "Take these!"

"That's not our bag, kid," Green says, trying to give them back.

"Mind telling me what you believe in?" the freak persists.

"I don't believe in miracles," Green replies. "I believe in what works."

The flippy white freak with the Afro hairdo smiles. "Would you believe how Christ works for me? I was a junkie for ten years . . . in every institution there is, trying to kick the habit. Then I met Jesus Christ. He turned my life around. Gave me *real* life. Never been on dope since." He looks at the two of them, first one, then the other, raises his finger, and says, "Praise God, brother. Jesus is real."

The two adults look at each other, then back at the freak.

IT'S GOOD TO KNOW

"Well, thank you," they say. They turn around and walk away. Under his breath as he looks at Mrs. Cole, Green says, "This *must* be the place!"

Cameras pan as they walk up the hill, and as they are walking a song with haunting melody and lyrics is heard — "I love you, I love you, I love you. . ."

The scene shifts to me as I stand on the hill-top in a blue shirt and glasses that look black in the sun. I say, "Well, we're sure talking about a lot of love around here today, people. But what is this love we talk about? It can mean anything from a deep, ecstatic feeling to something someone might say to someone else when they want to go to bed with them. The Bible says, in Luke 10, when Jesus was asked about love . . . He told them this story. . ."

The camera picks up Green and Mrs. Cole. Green says, "I don't think Jeff is here, Fran." They are about to turn and leave, when Mrs. Cole's eyes lock into mine as I say, "A man was traveling down the road from Jericho to Jerusalem, Jesus was saying, and he ran into some thieves who beat him up and took his clothes and money, left him there for dead at the roadside. A holy guy came by and saw him and decided it wasn't worth hassling about such a small problem and went on."

"An assistant from the temple," I continue relating Jesus' story, "saw him and he, also, thought the same thing. Didn't want to get involved. Now, people, that seems to be the human condition. Most of us are like that. We need, and reach out for this help, but everyone is too busy and passes us by."

By now, a lot of the people listening are in tears, and the mother for the first time is touched by spiritual feelings, the first in the family to be touched that way. The camera closes up on me, and I look tragic. "This isn't the end of the story," I say. "Another man came by, a despised Samaritan. You'd call him the last man to help because no one ever helped him. The Samaritans had their own ghetto and knew pain.

Yet, *this* man felt he should help the unfortunate one. He washed and bandaged him and cared for him."

Suddenly, as we were actually filming, there was a chink in the armor I'd built around myself. I blurted out, without thinking, but speaking as it leaped from somewhere deep within me, "Maybe some of you know what it is like to be waylaid by the side of life's highway. You felt the spirit of compassion. There is a lot of love here today. Jesus Christ is here with us. If you feel passed by, reach out and accept the love Jesus has to offer. Touch someone."

The music at this point swells up sadly and a collage scene is produced and Michelle comes up and puts her arm around the mother and Green, the "I love you" music continues to swell. . .

I kind of shuddered when I said the words, then the armor closed up again, and I shrugged, not caring from what mysterious spring within the lines had come. What difference could it make in my life? It was hard for me, now, to believe that Jesus brings love when I felt so unloved. On the last day of filming, I was already thinking about the roar of motorcycle engines and the Memorial Day classic TT race.

I said goodbye to my Hollywood friends after a short get-together with the people I knew at Hollywood Presbyterian Church. Of all that bunch, Don Williams was the only one who didn't give a nervous laugh when I told him about Karen. Don was about to be married. Maybe the seriousness of love helped him to understand. He looked at me. He knew I'd had bad times with women in the past. Quietly, he said, "What are you going to do?"

I hesitated, making sure the armor was locked securely in place. "The two people I loved the most just got married. I guess I have to give them my best wishes."

But I thought to myself then, and as I headed back to Colorado, this whole Christian thing, except perhaps for a few guys like Don Williams, is a gig. Well, at least I had

IT'S GOOD TO KNOW

launched a career, of sorts. Whatever might become of it, I didn't know. Maybe nothing.

I had told my boss I'd be back at work Saturday. Doug picked me up at the airport, and we went right to the shop. Then a weird thing happened to me. Without thinking, I picked up the receiver and put my finger in the dial. It was only then I realized I couldn't do it. I no longer could call and say, "I'm back, honey." That was in another script, the curtain had fallen.

The realization of what I'd almost done shook me. I felt disoriented.

I concentrated on the big race coming up. Doug and I would be in the main event. I knew my whole family would be there and probably Verne and Karen.

On the day of the race, Doug and I packed our bikes in his van and drove out early. We unloaded and talked to some of the other guys and gradually got our spirits revved up, as if we weren't already super revved.

For me, the race was a symbol — a coming back to something familiar, known — something I could depend on to give me identity. My old friend of years back and I were doing something we'd done — many, many times in the past. And, besides that, the race was a chance to show everyone I was worth something, that I still had life left in me.

Before I knew it, the loudspeaker commanded us to get on the starting line. Moving up, I felt at home and secure on my bike, fitting snugly, my hands curled around the handle grips.

Then . . . the starting signal. Everyone on either side of me, all of us at the same time, twisted the throttle, hit the gears — first . . . second . . . third . . . fourth . . . fifth. I was ripping up the straightaway, zooming into first place . . . then, first into the corner, going better than 90 miles an hour.

Approaching the corner, I threw the bike over sideways to

slow it down for the curve, sideways in that delicate, precarious position that takes all of one's concentration and skill.

Then . . . then I glanced up. And saw Karen and Verne. And wiped out.

Crashed.

As I lost control, time and space blurred. I did everything wrong. I let go of the bike, and it and I started tumbling across the ground, through the air, as if in slow motion. I rolled and hit the ground once, saw Karen again. The motorcycle bounced on me and I rolled again, still seemingly in slow motion as my mind somehow perceived things in agonizing detail . . . rolled, crashed, slammed down, came to a final stop.

At one point, when I was rolling, my arm bent under me and the bike hit me before I rolled again. Now that arm felt a little numb, but the pain hadn't started. I was somehow able to stumble to my feet and pick up my bike, as the roar of the other cycles, the excited yelling of the crowd and the anxious shouts of people running up to me all whirled around me dizzily.

Doug was at my side by the time I'd wheeled my bike part way to the van, and he helped me load it in. My parents finally came through the crowd as I lay down in the van and just mumbled at them. Verne and Karen came up to the door. "Go away," I moaned. It was hot. Someone suggested going to the hospital.

Why go to a hospital? I was hurt a lot worse deep inside and nobody suggested doing anything about that . . . showed any concern for that deep, deep wound that just went on throbbing.

No. I didn't want to go anywhere. I'd come to the races, and I wanted to stay here until they were over. The van radio was on, and I could follow the events, find out what was happening, who was on top.

I lay there until the races were over, lay there thinking

IT'S GOOD TO KNOW

how I had missed out while all around me guys were zinging around the turns and ripping up the straightaway.

Everyone was in the race but me.

As it turned out, my injuries weren't serious. My arm was hurt and useless for a while, but it wasn't really a big thing and as Spring tilted into Summer, I got back into the swing of biking, refusing to let go of the one thing left that had any meaning for me.

I worked hard all summer, working in the shop during the week, racing on Sundays. I didn't want any social life. My bike was my old lady and with everything taken into account, she was more trustworthy than the human variety. I loved my motorcycle! At least, she'd treat me exactly the way I guided her to treat me. Spills, crashes . . . those things happened through human error.

I hadn't spoken to Verne or Karen. After the crash, they went traveling. Verne had quit butchering and had gone back into singing and Karen went with him, on tours, appearances. Eventually, they got a house in Elizabeth, quite a distance from Denver, which pleased me; I couldn't stand the thought of seeing them together.

I was also speed mad! I wanted to do everything there was to do with my bike! I wanted to blot out the pain and the loss, my estrangement from God Himself, by speed and the sound of my bike and the wind in my face.

And I had a chance to challenge the very mountains! It was the 50th annual Pike's Peak Classic in Colorado Springs. My first race up a mountain! It would be a riproaring adventure in one of the world's hairiest races.

There were car and motorcycle events in this oldest auto race in the country, held on the fourth of July. Unser, Andretti — all the biggies were there. It started at 9,000 feet and went to the top of Pike's Peak — 14,110 feet, a 12½-mile climb over curving roads. You had to be geared for 100 mph.

I was in the last race of the day. It was usually sunny here at this time of the year, but not necessarily at the end of the run in this "Race to the Clouds." Today, from the start, the fog was deep, thick, and heavy. I wondered if there was any significance. "What's going on?" I wondered. "Is God or someone trying to chicken me out of this?"

Fat chance! I was working out a hurt and nothing Pike's Peak could do to me would be as bad as that hurt. During the day, I'd walked several miles up the mountain, as the cars barreled up, grinding and screeching and thundering. At each corner, I stopped, studied everything carefully, looked all around. I would get the jump on the others, I thought . . . memorize each corner, each dip or upward swing of the track. When I got a bearing on the first leg of the race from this walk-through inspection, I nodded in satisfaction. Bullock was using his brain again. I turned around and walked back down.

Finally, it was my race. There were 26 of us, in rows of six, on the starting line. I was confident. Besides having staked out a crucial part of the course, I had an amber shield to make visibility in the fog easier. As I waited for the flag to go down, my life wheeled before me in the drifting fog. I remembered that New York crash and the men with the white bloody coats. Well, it was going to be Pike's Peak or bust!

The prospect of the 12½-mile stretch on a dirt road, riding one of the 26 roaring big bikes with lots of horsepower in a dense fog, excited me. My pulses were thudding. Burning nitro, my Yamaha 360 was good for 100 miles an hour, and I knew it had enough horsepower to push us up those practically vertical walls leaning toward me. I knew that in many places, the roadside dropped straight down the mountain — a sheer drop — and if I miscalculated, I'd die for sure. I wasn't actually counting on coming in first, but I wanted to be in the running, and if I wasn't, well, maybe, it was just as well that I slid down into eternity along some rugged interface of those rocks.

Then the starter began to move the green flag in a circle, around and around, meaning GET READY. Whenever he dropped the flag, it would mean GO! I stared at him so hard he seemed to blur, and then, just as I was sure he was going to drop that flag, he blurred completely — backed off a little, right into the fog. He was out of sight, all right. A lump played yo-yo in my throat. I would have to wait for the bikes in front of me to sound off before I knew that the flag had fallen. It was pretty freaky.

Then it was like jets blasting in front of me and immediately the growl of my own engine mingled with the sounds that seemed to come from the mountain itself. I sat low and programmed my mind for the shape of the road I'd reconnoitered, giving the Yamaha everything it had. Then I was one of three in second spot. Number one was well ahead, in and out of the fog. I wanted to be where he was. I got right on the tail of the guy ahead of me on the fastest part of the course and stayed there, tailgating him like a hornet in pursuit.

I kept in the same position behind him for so long, presumably bobbing up and down in his rear view, that I finally unnerved him and he crashed in front of me at fantastic speed. I had to be quick to avoid hitting him. I pulled up on the handlebars and hoped I was going fast enough to jump over him. My back wheel left the road, all right, and there was just inches to spare, but I'd hit a rock just before jumping and my balance was off when I landed, and I ended up in a drainage ditch.

The gain I'd made from that was wiped out. As I fought to get out of that ditch, three bikes passed me.

But I did get out and stayed in the race, plunging upward as though I was falling in the wrong direction, slashing through waves of fog swirling across my path like the mountain's own panting breath.

Then, suddenly the road leveled off, the fog disappeared. I was above the clouds! Dead ahead was the finish line . . . while all spread out in every direction beneath me was the world waiting for just this moment.

I peered ahead, then swung a look around me. I'd won fifth place! Just enough to win a trophy! I'd come out of that drainage ditch, all right. I was on top of the world.

Again. I felt as if this ought to prove something.

Yet . . . yet as the next few weeks passed, I kept catching myself wondering why that victory seemed to be fading, falling behind me. Why couldn't I keep the same high? The excitement . . . it didn't last. The present became the past too quickly.

Was I to expect the bad things that had happened? It was strange. My accomplishments seemed too transitory . . . yet the tragedies of my life kept coming back to haunt me. Karen . . . Karen!

The frustration of not being able to do anything about the turmoil her name stirred in me made the bitterness and hate come back . . . hate for the ways people treat each other and the lies they tell about God, the way they use God as an excuse.

Just look ahead, I guess. Play out my part. Tomorrow and tomorrow and tomorrow creeps in this petty pace while all the time we poor mortals soup up our engines and vainly try to rush the future . . . which can only be death.

With the glow of my hill-climb faded, I had to look ahead and find my next big thrust somewhere in that dangerous land called the future. The next big race was coming up in a few weeks. For it Doug and I spent money like it was going out of style, putting our bikes in tiptop shape.

Meanwhile, for the past several months, I'd been having trouble with my wisdom teeth. I finally had to go to the dentist. I had to have some oral surgery; there was no way out of it. It would cost $150.

I was broke, and in a few days I would be having the expensive dental work. My boss picked this time to lay me off.

21

THE AFTERNOON of the surgery, I came home from the dentist feeling like a zombie, with six stitches in each jaw. Despite the pain pills which made me groggy, I was sicker than a dog. I had almost drifted off to sleep when the phone rang. "Whollo?" I said.

"Randy? Did I goof up on the time . . . you at dinner? Listen, Randy, this is Frank Jacobson. Your old exec producer at World Wide." He laughed. "I'm calling from Burbank, Rand. You've got to get out here. Right away. We have to reshoot your scene."

"What do you mean, reshoot it?"

"We'll explain all that when you get out here. Do you still remember all your lines? Do you still have those funny little dark glasses?"

"Yeah. I still have my funny little dark glasses . . . ow!" It hurt to talk!

"Well, bring those dark glasses and the blue shirt, and we'll fake it."

"Frank, I just had mouth surgery, and I can't go anywhere."

"You have to! We hired a whole crew and staked out the location for shooting in two days. You've got to get here."

As we'd talked, I kept thinking, "It's a job, it's a job."

IT'S GOOD TO KNOW 207

The timing as far as the dental work was concerned was way out in deep space, but I could use the bread.

"I . . . I don't have enough money for a ticket at the moment," I said, wanting to establish the money question right off, as well as wanting to tell the whole truth and nothing but.

"We'll pay the air ticket from this end, no sweat," Jacobson said. "All you have to do is be on the plane. We'll even have someone meet you at this end." He hesitated, then went on — "If you're worred about money kid, naturally you'll get paid. There's at least two days involved, plus expenses."

I hustled around, got on my bike and zoomed downtown just in time to catch my dentist before he closed up. I explained the situation. The dentist loaded up a needle and advanced on me. "This will keep the swelling down and it shouldn't be too noticeable. A good jolt of cortisone in your lower jaw, and with this codeine pills for the pain. . ."

I just held myself together for the next few hours and then I was on a plane, then landing. At the airport, someone I didn't know met me and drove me out to Sportsman's Lodge in Studio City. It was around ten o'clock at night. I was sick and running a fever. I did manage to sleep, but when the phone woke me the next morning I felt even worse. "We'll be picking you up in half an hour," a voice said. "Wanted you to know so you could grab a bite to eat."

"Oh, sure. Eat, eh?" Breakfast was the last thing I felt like. After hanging up the phone, I grabbed a couple of the pills. By the time they escorted me to the car, I was not only sick and running a fever, I was goofy in the head from all the codeine.

Kenette Riggs, Bill Brown, President of World Wide Pictures, Cliff Barrows, Chairman of the Board of World Wide, and I went on location.

On the way, Cliff went over some changes in the lines he wanted me to make. I wasn't thinking very straight, but I managed to program it all into my mind some way. Then I had to stand on top of a hill the rest of the day, and do my lines, going through several takes before they were satisfied. I felt that for a second time on the same assignment, I had been waylaid by the side of life's highway. I had trouble getting anything straight. I could anticipate people coming up to me after the film was shown and saying, "Man, you look like you were really hurt in that scene."

For the next two months after I got back home I waited around in limbo, then finally landed a job working for a high pressure water/steam industrial cleaning establishment. But I soon tired of the whole scene and laid plans to join a friend, Ryan Moses, in Santa Barbara, California, after Christmas and, presumably, after the world premiere of *Time To Run.*

Verne and Karen had taken off on another cross-country singing tour and Wayne had gotten a job in Carson City, Nevada. My parents and I had a quiet Christmas, but it was the nicest in several years for me, as far as being with my family was concerned.

I'd been waiting and waiting to hear from World Wide Pictures about the premiere, and early in January, 1972, I finally called them. "We still don't know," Jacobson said. "Sorry. We'll let you know in a few days."

When I didn't hear by January 17, I told my parents, "I don't even know World Wide!" I got into my Simca and split.

I hadn't had time to scope out my new beauty spot by the seaside in Santa Barbara when, on January 21, I got a telegram, re-directed from Denver — "Urgent you call Chuck Wenger Holiday Inn Memphis Tennessee immediately."

I called. "Where in the world are you, Randy?" Chuck said.

"*Who* in the world are you?" I countered.

"Who? Me?" He laughed. "I'm one of the management

IT'S GOOD TO KNOW

people at World Wide in Minneapolis. I'm the guy that buzzes around buying theater time, setting up showings. Anyway, listen, I thought someone had been in touch with you, but, anyway, can you get to Memphis, right away?"

"Memphis?"

"Yes, for the world premiere."

"How long are you going to keep me?"

"Four days . . . maybe longer. We'd like to have you appear at some of the openings in Minnesota, too." He paused, then continued — "All expenses and a little spending money, too, Randy. Someone will be at the airport to meet you. A room will be reserved for you at the Rivermont Hotel. Can you do it?"

"Sure, sure," I said. He sounded as if he was in a hurry, and I had to be, too, to do that.

Nobody was at the airport to meet me in Memphis. Some firemen were there because the airport was on fire. I charged my way through the mass confusion and had to stand on my head to get attention. Wearing a blue denim shirt open at the neck over a brown striped polo shirt, old jeans with a wide leather belt, and brown boots, I didn't appear prosperous enough for the taxi drivers to think of fat tips, but I finally stood in front of one. "Rivermont Hotel!" I shouted, jumping in, "and hurry."

He turned around and looked at me. "You're kidding."

"No. Hurry."

"You sure you can pay for it?"

I opened my billfold and showed him the lonely ten-dollar bill tucked neatly in there.

"That's what it'll take, buddy," he said, revving out into the street and driving like a comet.

At the hotel a room had been reserved and paid for in my name, but none of the people I asked for were in. I wandered around the hotel, walked around the block, then came back into the lobby and saw Randall Carver, one of the stars.

As I went to speak to him, I ran into a guy in a tuxedo, with a big flower in his lapel.

"You're Randy Bullock, aren't you? I'm Chuck. I called you, remember?" He smiled. "On your way to the theater. . .? Know where it is? You all set up okay?"

"If it's in walking distance," I said. "First, I was going to rent a tux. . ."

"Aw, go like you are, Rand. It'll add a little color. Uh, by the way, you will ride to the theater in the limo with Mr. Brown, Joan Winmill, Tedd Smith and the other stars."

It was a little different watching myself in a movie that was a regular feature-length story, as opposed to the documentaries I'd been in. I didn't actually look inappropriate with my rather immobile mouth in the preaching sequence. I looked worn with care, and I smiled, now, thinking how sometimes adversity turns itself into advantage even without one's efforts. I was really up in orbit over the big, enthusiastic, and appreciative crowd attending the showing.

In all the excitement of the moment, some of the bitterness that had soured me for the past several months was suspended. I felt aglow, on the brink of a new life, in my real element.

At the reception after the film, at the hotel, Bill Walton, a Holiday Inns executive and premiere general chairman for Memphis, stood with repressed excitement evident on his face. "I have a very special announcement," he said. Then, in a rush — "President Nixon has just announced a ceasefire in Vietnam."

Everybody went wild. There was screaming, handclapping, and "Praise the Lord's" for ten or fifteen minutes. When Walton finally restored order, Pastor R.P. Caudill interrupted, "I think this is time for a prayer of thanksgiving. And also a reason to sing 'All Hail the Power of Jesus' Name.' " We bowed our heads and then, a few moments later, the song burst out load and clear, and I was full of tears I didn't know the source of.

IT'S GOOD TO KNOW

It was a double whammie for me, considering my hate of the war and my brief touch with God's grace . . . restored, now, at least momentarily by the thundering wave of emotion.

World Wide officials, including Bill Brown, President of World Wide, and his wife, came to the mike to make speeches. The stars were introduced one by one and given a few minutes for comments.

When it was my turn, Bill Brown said, "I'm glad Randy came dressed like this. He is simply being himself, without any pretense. Yet his Christian testimony comes through very clearly."

I was whammied again. People were throwing challenges at me . . . things to live up to. I felt humbled and ashamed of the weaknesses and hate that had been rekindled in me, and the idea of the end of the war, the restoration of some measure of peace, intensified these feelings. "Put yourself in my shoes," I said to the group. "From way back, I have been a crusader against the war and repressive politics and unquestioned conformity. I reacted in some violent and unsavory ways and didn't help the cause for peace any in the doing. But it was strange — it was this very road in life that brought me to Jesus Christ and that path brought me to this fantastic night, this film and this big stuff. It is ironic that it is this very night that President Nixon has announced the end of the war."

There was applause and cheers, and I felt for a moment that I'd had a leading role in this play. At the end of the evening, I took a last look at the elegant ballroom and the well-dressed people, and despite all that had happened, I felt a little sad. My parents would have loved this. I was a little peeved at the poor planning or whatever it was that had made it impossible for them to attend. It would have been the highlight of their lives.

I was tired and emotionally drained and slept hard all night. In the morning, a loud rapping on my door woke me up. It was Chuck Wenger. "Hurry and get dressed. You're late."

"For what? Breakfast?"

"No. The plane to Minneapolis. It leaves right away. Hurry, hurry, hurry."

I sighed. "Chuck, you guys should tell me when I'm going to be flying and I can be ready."

"Sorry about that. Again. Anyway, I'll wait for you in the lobby. And you'll be met in Minneapolis and maybe things will start happening on time. I hope. I just work here too. . ."

When I got down to the lobby, Chuck introduced me to a Bud Levy, President of Translux, one of the several exhibitors who'd attended the premiere. As we drove to the airport, our conversation was interrupted when Chuck pointed out the place where Martin Luther King had been assassinated. For a moment, I was taken back in time to when I'd first heard about the shooting. I remembered how bitter I'd felt then about the hate all around — yet how I'd supported this very kind of violence. I thought about southern people, and how polite both whites and blacks are in the South, bound together in a sort of cultural symbiosis. I felt even now that some of the sins ascribed to the South by the North were exaggerated. Our biggest problem in the United States seemed to me that we were united but segmented off into regions.

At the airport, Mr. Levy, talking a mile a minute telling me how much he liked *Time To Run* and my part in it, walked me right up to the door of my plane. "Next time you're in New York," he said, "be sure to look me up. I'm at 635 Madison Avenue."

The name rang a bell. It was the address of the building where the Roast Beef and Brew Restaurant was located, an address which included a number of magazine publishers and important people.

I said goodbye and settled into a seat and thought about

IT'S GOOD TO KNOW

the reminders of the past that had assailed me since I'd arrived in Memphis. I had to make up my mind about things. Either I was going to play this Jesus Christ thing straight and honestly, at least doing my best at it, or I should be back down in the streets throwing bottles. I tried to pray. It struck me that praying was coming hard. I realized then that it takes practice and continuous trying to hold onto one's commitments. Who could I talk to for help? I felt utterly alone.

Nobody was at the air terminal to meet me when I landed in Minneapolis. I had no idea where I was to go or whom to contact. I waited in the waiting room. And waited. There were hundreds of people milling around, sitting, waiting for flights or meeting people from flights. I was beginning to get desperate, wondering what I should do next. Finally, after an hour, my name was called on the intercom and at the desk I met Dan Churchill. "I was delayed," was all he said.

Dan took me to a hotel to get checked in, then took me to see several of the staff. "We don't know exactly what to do with you at this point," someone named Andy said, "but you can help with the publicity."

I had just been returned to my hotel, cleaned up, and had a bite to eat, when Dan Churchill found me again. "Andy has decided to give you a little job. He wants you to speak at nine churches here in the next few days."

"Oh."

Dan laughed. "Here's a list of the churches and their addresses. I'll take you to the car rental agency. . ."

"Car rental?"

"So you can get to the churches."

At the National Car Rental Agency, I nearly fell over when a guy impeccably suited and looking VIP rushed out of an office with some keys in his hand. I looked around. All the semi-mini-skirted girls in the salesroom were looking on with wide-open mouths. "I'm Vince Abrahmson," the man introducing himself said as he pumped vigorously on my hand, "president of the company. I'm so very pleased to meet you." He grinned broadly. "It's not often I get to meet a Hollywood star."

"Oh, yeah, of course," I said, at a loss for words.

"I suppose they told you I'm a Christian and have supported World Wide Pictures and other Billy Graham activities."

"Well, actually, no, they didn't," I said. "Frankly, they don't brief me very well."

"Well, well, well, I'm so glad we can help you," Abrahmson said. "I've picked out one of our late-model sporty cars for your use. Sorry, but all the 73's are out." He handed me the keys. I wasn't sure if I could handle the vehicle. I was afraid I'd be so unnerved I might end up hitting a light pole.

I thanked him and drove off to the hotel parking lot. I wanted a cup of coffee and a chance to come down out of orbit.

Here I was, with a few pennies in my pocket, and a hot '72 to gad about in. The hotel was nice, too, of course. Besides, it was the only place I could eat where I could put it on the cuff.

On the list of churches were some notes to guide me in what to say and how long to talk, but they left it mostly up to me. I contacted the various pastors by telephone and confirmed the times given on the list, then quickly roughed out some remarks.

My reception was good. Fortunately, my speech and drama background had prepared me for meeting any kind of audience under almost any circumstances.

This kept me busy for three or four days, and it was climaxed by a talk at Northwestern Bible School and College, of which Billy Graham was President around 20 years ago, when he and his associates first conceived the idea for an evangelical movement.

I'd come full circle. Here I was, on a college campus again, talking to young people. In the past I had spoken

IT'S GOOD TO KNOW 215

words of hate and violence and advocated free love, free drugs, and free sin. Now I was using my experiences as an example of what these freedoms in a selfish context can do to groups, individuals and nations. "Love is the answer," I told them.

Later, as I sat in the living room of Dan Churchill's house, I got to thinking that *I* still needed to talk with someone to iron out this love thing. Until I understood how love and Jesus could be the answer to hurt feelings and bleeding bodies, my words would ring hollow in my own ears.

Dan had been talking to Andy on the phone, while I was trying to piece it together. Suddenly, he turned to me. "Andy wants to talk to you."

I grabbed the phone. "Hi, Andy," I said. "I've been doing a lot of talking these past few days, and I think maybe I ought to cool it awhile —"

"Listen, Randy, you won't believe it! You're going to speak in front of 7,000 people this Saturday. It's a big Lutheran Mid-Winter Youth Conference. Isn't that terrific? Uh, what were you saying when you picked up the phone?"

"Never mind," I sighed. "Tell me more." It seemed everything was out of my hands.

"Well, listen. There's another Bullock who's going to be there. A singer from Colorado. You wouldn't know him, would you?"

"No. I don't know him." I held my hand over the mouthpiece and chuckled wryly. He'd caught me by surprise, conflicting feelings were swirling in me. Well, it would be a little bit of fun to surprise Verne by my presence there. Whatever other feelings might be aroused, at least maybe the surprise would lighten the mood.

When I got to the conference, I was told that Verne would have half an hour for singing and that I would introduce him. After his part in the program, I would say a few words to the group and that would be that. I knew I was nervous and a short speech suited me just fine.

It was hard for me to decide whether or not I should regard this as a chance for Verne and me to get back together again and let by-gones be by-gones, or as a challenge. I was in a flux. I had been trying to resurrect love in my soul, but the acid drip of memory kept eating away at my heart.

As Verne's time drew near, and he still hadn't shown up, I started wondering. My brother was always prompt, usually ahead of time. I began to worry that something had happened. The guys on the platform were also beginning to worry, for different reasons.

Then as we all sat there in growing anxiety, with the audience beginning to sense that something had gone wrong, a liaison man came running up the aisle, waving a piece of paper.

My heart skipped a beat. "Something's happened to Verne!" I thought.

The liaison man handed the paper to the man at the mike. A strange look flitted across the M.C.'s face. He squared up with the mike and said, "This is not the kind of announcement that is easy to make."

I sank in my chair. I felt cold. My heart was hammering a mile a minute. My throat was dry.

"President Nixon has just announced there is no longer going to be any draft."

I just about keeled over in my chair. Wow. Another double whammie — this time half of it, at least, being great news. A good omen! There was a general sigh, a pause, then yelping and whooping and hand-clapping, people standing up and cheering and praising the Lord. A few bars of song burst out, then the man at the mike said, "Let's silently offer our thanks at this moment. . ."

Everyone bowed their heads and for two or three minutes that vast auditorium was deathly quiet . . . as a tribute to life!

Verne still hadn't appeared. After the prayer, someone

IT'S GOOD TO KNOW 217

came up to me and said, "Look, why don't you just go ahead and speak for that half hour?"

"Look, what do you think I am?"

But he'd already turned around and retreated from my protests and before I could think, my name was coming over the mike and everyone was looking in my direction. I went up to the stage and spoke.

I mentioned yet again how I'd been a partner with rabble-rousers, how I'd been kicked out of the University of Colorado, photographed as a participant in the May Day disturbance, and tripped with pot and peyote, with LSD in between. "After all that hate and anger," I said, "I ended up watching myself die in New York. And, I did die there! Because the man you see now was reborn in Wichita. . ." I had to swallow some lumps as the thought hit me that I wished I had also died in Wichita, at this high point in my salvation, before I found out that being a Christian isn't the end to trouble, after all. "But God does not promise us a rose garden, either . . . unless we lean firmly on Him. . ."

I was conscious that I was beginning to answer my own question, the question I'd had about how you keep loving, when you are going under and feel trampled and oppressed.

Maybe if I'd been able to talk another half hour, I'd have worked out that answer fully. Or else broken down! As it was, I felt too jittery as the end of my speech neared, and I waved at them, stuck my finger in the air, and said, "Jesus is love!"

I sat down to big cheers and thought back over some of the things I'd said so automatically, inspired by God, surely, as He spoke through me. I realized I'd expressed another pregnant thought; I'd been concerned for Verne's safety. I'd explained how tense I was when that liaison man had come running down the aisle. I did love Verne, then, a whole lot more than I thought. Yet, I . . . I also hated him. Or hated what he did.

I shook my head. It was so confusing. I was starting to

worry again about him, regardless of how much I hated him, when, as the meeting was coming to an end, Verne strolled in with his guitar. People were already beginning to disperse. Verne looked around, spotted me, and fought his way through the crowd. "Are they coming or going?" he asked.

"You're slightly late. How come?" I asked.

Verne shrugged. "They just said to come by some time this morning. I didn't know things got started so early. . ."

I laughed. "They seem to have a habit in my organization too, of neglecting to fill one in on the details. Hey, but how come you didn't fall over in a faint when you saw me? I thought you'd say, 'Man, it's a small world, all right!' "

Verne cocked his head and raised his eyebrows. "Why should I? Some guy named Andy called Lutheran Evangelical and said you'd be there. Wasn't I suppose to know?"

I shrugged. "Well, I was planning for it to be a big surprise." I thought, some people seem to be able to pull off surprises.

"Another thing they didn't do," Verne said, "is leave me with any money. Oh, well. . ."

"Well, come for a spin in my cruiser and I'll feed you at the hotel. Where are you staying by the way?"

"At the 'Y'."

"Oh."

We went to the hotel and had lunch and talked about what we'd been doing. He was touring the country again, Jesus style, and I was glad, despite myself, that he'd put himself back together again. Then I took him back to the Y.M.C.A. and it was only as we parked that I finally broached the subject of Karen.

"How . . . is she?" I murmured.

"Pregnant," he replied. "The baby's due in August."

The next day or so, I took it easy. I'd been keyed up more than I realized talking with Verne and thinking about Karen, and I was uncomfortable again, feeling a little sorry for myself.

By then, some of the "bigger guns" of World Wide had arrived in Minneapolis to discuss my fate, as well as other plans for the promotion of *Time To Run,* and I was elected to chauffeur Randy Carver and Barbara Sigel around town.

Shortly after I'd performed this task, feeling a little like a flunky and wondering how my vast experience in publicity had earned me only this mediocre role, Chuck Wenger got together with me. He laughed. "I'm sorry I had you do that, Randy."

"Why in particular?" I asked, agreeing with him.

"Because I always know when Ken Bliss is uptight with me. He calls me Charles. He came up to me and said, 'Charles, what's Randy doing?' 'Randy's driving Randy and Barbara around,' I answered. 'Well, Charles, that's a terrific waste of talent.' "

I nodded.

"Sorry about that. We'll give you more interesting things to do."

"Good. Only—." I struggled for words. "I'm having a rough time, Chuck. Can't get my own self put together. . ."

Chuck looked at me thoughtfully for a while without speaking. Then, "I can see it. Something's repressed. You're holding something in."

Now I was chicken. When the opportunity presented itself to talk about it, I was afraid. Proud and afraid. "I don't want to talk about it."

Chuck laughed. "That just makes me want to hear about it even more. Come on, Randy. We're friends in Christ." Chuck was really showing an interest in my problems.

I opened my mouth to say something, then closed it again, as I suddenly choked. I felt as though I was caving in. I turned my head away quickly as tears filled my eyes. It was no use trying to stop them before Chuck saw. Finally, I calmed down and said, "You knew my brother, Verne, the singer. Well, I was engaged to a girl named Karen. . ." I took a deep breath. "As far as I knew, everything was beautiful. Then, out of the blue. . ."

I described the rest of the situation, and Chuck said, "You wanted Karen more than anything in the world? Listen, Randy, you have two tasks to perform. Get right with God, first. Just pray for forgiveness. Do you know what you did, Randy, in the way you regarded this girl?"

I hated to confess it, but I saw what Chuck was driving at. "Putting Karen above God?" My words were all shaky. The mere mention of her name. . .

"Pray for forgiveness for not putting Jesus first."

"And to forgive me for saying I hated God!" I could hardly say it as tears came to my eyes again and my voice shook.

"Ask God to bless the whole Verne and Karen relationship. And, Randy, more than that," Chuck continued. "What you'd better do is ask God to share this burden of pain with you."

"Will you pray with me?" I was humble now, after all the thoughts I'd had earlier about being just a flunky and thinking I deserved more.

"Yes, I will. But one other thing — the second thing; call Verne and Karen. Or write to them. Tell them you forgive them Randy, and that you love them, too."

Way back in ancient times, in Wichita, far away in time, I had come to the decision on my own to tell my father I loved him. I'd based this on the insight that love wasn't much good if not shared. "Yeah, I know you're right," I said. "You know, though, I found out just a while ago I still love my brother. I wasn't sure for a while. But when I thought something had happened to him. . ."

"There are two forces struggling in each of us," Chuck said. "Let's pray about it."

We bowed our heads, and I took a deep breath and said, "God, forgive me for hating You. And Verne. And Karen." I prayed silently, repeating the prayer over and over, and each time I felt a little calmer. There was just one resistance my stubborn heart offered. I knew I could forgive Karen and Verne, and that I truly did love them despite the bitter hurt. But I wasn't so sure I could tell them, or even say it in a letter.

There came to me more vividly the conviction that I had coveted the relationship with Karen and the thought of having a wife even more than God. God seemed right now to tell me that He'd taken away that marriage with Karen to teach me the error. At the very same time, He had rewarded me with this chance with World Wide Pictures. Right on the very day that I was flying to California for the filming, they were getting married. It was so clear.

Suddenly, God also seemed to remind me of my own words when I presented Verne with the new guitar I'd raised money for. I'd told the story of how a man was punished for worshipping his guitar more than God.

We were kneeling, and I was shaking as I prayed, my eyes closed, but I felt the radiation of Chuck being near me and my mind went back in time. I remembered how Verne had saved my life in New York when he'd called and invited me to come to Wichita. He'd saved two lives, really — my physical life and my spiritual life. In the most important ways, Verne had given.

And I saw how selfish I'd been with Karen, using her savings and then, when God brought some money our way, blowing the whole bundle on myself, without calling her or even thinking of her or our future. Was that love? Not Jesus' kind. All the "hurt" that I'd been nursing — nurturing was more like it — was nothing more than a wounded ego. And that caused me to think of a rush of other times that I'd been so completely caught up in myself that I'd been utterly insensitive to the feelings of those around me. All that mattered was *my* thoughts, *my* needs, *my* emotions . . . And

I began to see what a monumental ego-trip my whole life had been...

There was more, too much to even consciously acknowledge, though my heart knew what was happening; God, in His mercy, was giving me a gift of repentance — a heart of flesh for a heart of stone. And the more clearly I saw who I was — who I *really* was — the more I knew how much I needed Jesus.

"Lord, I'm a mess, clear through. Everything I touch, I seem to mess up. And still you love me." I started to cry. "Forgive me, Lord, and help me to change." The last was scarcely a whisper.

22

I FELT A WEIGHT off my spirit immediately. I felt ten years younger, a new person, inside and out! A deep spiritual healing and cleansing had taken place.

There was more. I'd thanked God for giving me the start with World Wide Pictures, and the next day the staff had finally decided what they were going to do with me. "We want you to drive through Minnesota and make appearances at eight cities Randy," Chuck said.

The Lord blessed my appearances. It was a new experience, being an ambassador for Christ, and He gave me the words and the inspiration. It was a different kind of thrill, too, to see people's eyes light up, and to know that Randy Bullock had had nothing to do with it.

All I could do was be obedient to the leading I sensed and trust God to take it from there. And when people would come up afterwards to congratulage me, I would simply say, "Praise the Lord! He did it, not me!"

It would take another book to tell just the highlights of what happened during the next nine months while on tour promoting *Time To Run* for World Wide Pictures. But a few things have to be recorded here.

In Philadelphia I had a chance to speak at the Media Detention Center. I was told when I arrived that I would have an hour if I wanted, but that I would be lucky to hold their attention for five minutes. These were supposed to be the nastiest, rottenest little teenagers in town, and nobody, especially anybody with any form of religious instruction, could ever speak to them for more than five minutes without getting spitwads thrown at them. They told me that the last Christian they had had was a singer, and he was pretty good. He had lasted a whole seven minutes, and that was a new record.

Forewarned, I prayed before going out to talk with them. I knew these kids wouldn't get a chance to see *Time To Run*, and I wanted to present Jesus to them. I started by telling them where I'd been in my life, the problems I'd had. Then I told them about *love,* His kind, not man's . . . time got away from us, and we got a little discussion going and were there for an hour and a half! We had to cancel dinner.

One of the guards, a big black man who was about 6'6", came up to me afterwards and said, "Can't you stay?"

I had to tell him I was sorry, but we were scheduled for another place that night. I was still thinking about the little girl who had stood up and had dared to ask me a question. She was pretty, dark, and Spanish-looking. I could see needle marks on her arms, and she was pregnant. She was crying when she asked, "Do you think Jesus Christ can cure what a heroin addict has?"

"I don't know," I told her, "but Jesus was the same man that raised Lazarus from the dead, cured the sick, fed five thousand people, turned water into wine. . ." and I went on naming a few more miracles they probably hadn't heard of. Then I said, "He probably considers heroin a drop in the bucket." And I grinned, as hope began to light up her eyes.

I also told the teenagers I was going on to Texas the next week, and when I said this I noticed quite a change came over them. One fellow even started to cry. So I asked them,

IT'S GOOD TO KNOW

"What does Texas mean to you?"

There was a babble of voices, but I could make out their answers as, "Sky... land... water... streams... air." One teenager kept shouting, "Prairie!" That's all he would say. Finally I got him to talk some more, and he said he had read about Brownwood, Waco, and a few other places. He said he wanted the space the prairie could offer. He said he thought he could be free somewhere like that and wouldn't have to steal. I told them I hadn't heard of those places in Texas, but I would thank God for them when I got there.

A couple of days later while still in Philadelphia, I had to speak at the Landsdale High School, a brand new building that had cost taxpayers well in excess of 10 million dollars. When I walked in, the atmosphere was oppressive. Instead of having the hour I'd planned, the Principal said I would have five minutes and in that five minute period of time I was told not to mention God.

I guess they didn't want any taxpayers calling up afterwards and complaining about someone preaching to their kids. Funny, taxpayers don't seem to mind paying for preachers to go into the prisons, after the fact!

I said to those kids, "I've been asked to tell you everything I know about life in five minutes and told that what I'm going to tell you is against the law." As I said this I noted some of the administrators were sunk down in the back seats as if they were afraid. Then I went on to say, "What I would really like to tell you about is what God did for me! and my life! Beginning with the fact that I wouldn't be here to tell you about it if it was not for Him. But I can't say that here." The best I could do for them was to say, "If you would like to know more about this, go see our movie, *Time To Run.*"

When I was through in Philadelphia, it was onto Amarillo for a day, where I met Russell Carver, the father of Randy Carver, who played the main part in *Time To Run*. We just had a few moments to chat, but I arranged to meet him when I came back through.

When I got back to Dumas, Texas, I called the master of ceremonies for the local Lion's Club. "You'll have about three minutes," the guy said hurriedly on the phone. "Just three minutes?" I sputtered. "I've come all this way to talk to 200 people, you say, for three minutes?"

"Look, we don't want to hear about God, we just want to hear about this movie, and when it's coming to town. Okay?"

I simmered down. "Okay, I'll be there."

As soon as I hung up, I prayed. I asked God to forgive me for being so uptight with this man. After all, he had to schedule a program. They probably hadn't told him I was prepared to speak longer. As soon as I stopped praying, the phone in my hotel room rang.

"Mr. Bullock, this is the M.C. for the Lion's Club. Our entertainment for the day just cancelled out. Do you think you could take the whole 45 minutes?"

I had a 16 minute promotional clip from *Time To Run* with me. I said, "Have you got a projector?"

"Yes, sir."

"Okay, then I'll be there." I hung up and said, "Thank you, Lord!"

When I got back to Amarillo, I was supposed to meet Russell Carver at his bank at 3 p.m. I waited and waited but he didn't come. Finally I went inside and asked about him. He had been in a car accident and they told me what hospital he had been taken to. By the time I got there, he was talking about the accident. "Everything is in God's hands, Randy. The reason I had that wreck was so I could tell the woman who hit me about Jesus. When you've got God on your side, who can be against you?"

We said a little prayer together and he gave me best wishes for the rest of my tour. I was scheduled to leave Amarillo and start hitting towns in the great wide prairie.

Great things happened in those little towns. I found out I was going to be in Brownwood, Texas, on my birthday,

IT'S GOOD TO KNOW

March 18, to speak at a State correctional girl's school.

When I pulled into Brownwood, there was a giant *Time To Run* poster signed by a couple of hundred people from West Chester, Pennsylvania. It said, "We love you, Randy." I had no idea how it got to me on my birthday. "Brownwood," I said to myself. "This is the place that teenager told me he would like to be. I had better look around and appreciate it for him."

The next day when I drove from Brownwood to Waco, I remembered those teenagers again and I stopped along the way to pray and appreciate what they had said about the prairie being so beautiful.

When I spoke in the Austin area, I couldn't help but feel I was speaking to the little brothers and sisters of the teenagers I had turned on to LSD earlier. I had come back into an area where I had caused trouble before. Now I was bringing God's message.

The Governor of Texas had declared a *Time To Run* Week and had urged all of the citizens of Texas to see the movie. This helped me on my tour, and when I approached San Antonio and was looking for the Ramada Inn, I happened to glance up and there was a big sign saying, "Welcome Randy Bullock, Co-star of *Time To Run*." These Texans never let you down.

This spurred me on for the last two places in Texas, Brownsville and Corpus Christi. I spoke at a high school in Brownsville and for 55 minutes I had their complete attention. Even nods and smiles. Then the principal stood up and said, "Excuse me, Mr. Bullock, but did you know that nobody here speaks English?"

In Corpus Christi, all the publicity had said it would be Randy Carver coming, so I thanked them and apologized, and said I would do my best.

Randy's father, Russell Carver, had just died from complications of the broken hip he had gotten in his accident. No one had expected this. I talked to Randy after hearing the news and I tried to console him. He felt badly about not seeing him before he died and I told him the conversation we had had in the hospital. This seemed to help Randy when I kept repeating the last thing I had remembered him saying, "I'm not worried, I'm in God's hands."

From Texas, I flew into Wisconsin and was taken to the university campus in Madison. Students had driven around the campus with a public address system saying, "What did Abbie Hoffman do for you, what did the SDS do for you, come and hear Randy Bullock speak!"

That night it was snowing and the militant Jews turned out to disrupt my speech, but I didn't give them a chance.

From Madison we went to Green Bay, and then to Two Rivers, Wisconsin, where I was told to call the chairman's home as soon as I got in. But I was late and when I called, no one answered. I drove around town, hoping for an answer, saying, "I need help, God. Where is this meeting?" The first thing I saw was the police station and I pulled in there like gang busters. I said, "Do you know where I'm supposed to be?"

The guy looked up, looked at me kind of strangely, then said, "Yeah, follow me."

I had a police escort to the local high school which I never would have found. I got there as the people were singing. I guess the Lord wanted me to be sure and make this meeting because the chairman's brother was there and he needed counseling help.

From Wisconsin I was to make another big jump — to Pittsburgh. I had arrived dead-tired, and it was only by the grace of God that I was able to get through an unbelievable schedule. The capper was a 10 a.m. meeting at a school for deaf children. I talked to a group of 11th graders who were some of the most beautiful kids I had ever seen. I acknowledged my handicap to them, and asked through my interpreter, who was making hand signals, if we could accept for one another a different form of communication.

"I've always felt audio and verbal communications is one of the most deficient forms of communication we have," I said.

They agreed.

"By all means, allow me to suggest *love*."

"Love?" They all nodded.

"Or spirit, or sense?"

"Okay."

I began to speak. During the whole tour, I had never told the story of the Good Samaritan. Since it is played up in a very dramatic way in the film, I had always thought it would be too easy to use. But for these kids at the deaf school, I sensed it might be appropriate. Slowing down to give my interpreter time to make all the signals, I told the story with *love*. Some read my lips. I told them what Jesus Christ could do for them, and what He had already done for me.

Then I told them about the movie and when I finished, they promised me they would go see *Time To Run*, and I promised them that they would be able to hear it.

We had formed a bond in communications. I went away with a strange and wonderful feeling, not caring whether I had had any sleep for the past twenty-four hours. My own personal problems were small compared to theirs.

Again, I thanked God, for what He had taught me through them.

Epilogue

My World Wide Pictures travels were only the beginning of a whirlwind tour in the Spirit which was akin to a traveling ministry, and I fulfilled Acts 1:8, "But ye shall receive power, when the Holy Spirit is come upon you: and shall be my witnesses both in Jerusalem and in all Judea and Samaria, and into the uttermost part of the earth."

With new life, and real love prayerfully channeled through Jesus Christ this time, I began experiencing tremendous growth of the Spirit. I felt I was traveling vertically more than I could ever travel horizontally around the wide world.

I recalled often the mountain peak in Colorado, standing with my father, watching the eagle soar and wanting to be free as a bird. Now I felt free, liberated from anchoring my feelings on transitory, temporal things, instead, letting love through Christ lift me, soaring.

Now I could see some of the things which had bogged me down before. In the talks I had made throughout the country, I had many times said what I now saw as the reason for so much misery and fighting in our country and the world. Reality without Christ was unbearable. Young people would do anything to avoid looking at the Big Zero in their lives. Sex. Kids saw it on TV and replicated it in junior high, high school, and college. Kids had seen and done everything by

IT'S GOOD TO KNOW 231

the time they were 18. Then, there they were; they'd crossed all of life's thresholds and were like 90-year-olds in experience.

No wonder they became depressed. No wonder they turned to dope and tried for a new high. They'd lived such a full life that they'd bored themselves stiff by the time they were teenagers. No wonder they blew their minds. Dope was only a symptom of their problems. Booze, sex, boredom; all of these were symptoms. Political radicalism and violence were symptoms. Symptoms of a desperate escape from having to face the Grim Reaper, the Great Despair.

Instead of trying to treat symptoms, such as witchcraft, alcoholism, addiction, I was now on fire to tell people to get at the cause. Jesus is the opposite of a void, and as empty as life is without Him, life *with* Him is so full, it runneth over. I was doing my best to get people to try it and see. My own life was proof positive of that.

And when I spoke to those who already knew Him, and knew that what I said was true, I shared a little of what He was teaching me. Like in Romans, it tells us not to look for God or His Will, or ask for it, but to know it. Present your body as a living holy sacrifice to the Lord. Refuse to conform to the ways of the world. Be transformed by a renewing of the mind and spirit. Then you will become what is good and pleasing and perfect, and you will instinctively know the Will of the Lord.

Some of the people I spoke to replied, "Oh, I look so hard for the Will of the Lord!" I answered each time, "You've already got it. When God says jump, you don't say, why, or how high or do I have to right now? You jump, because it's the Will of God and you don't question it. God's Will is three inches in front of your nose, yet people are blinded by the fact that it is so close, and they strain themselves looking off into the distance. God's *inside* you!"

As I talked hundreds of times in big and little places all over the U.S., promoting *Time To Run*, which appealed in its own way for more love in lives, I continued to learn and grow in Jesus Christ. Now, at last, I felt truly useful in the highest sense . . . a real instrument of God, symbol of a life running full circle, right through the eye of Japetas into negative space and out the other end again, back into positive love and infinite glory. His.

Verne and I were both doing the same thing during this period of time. Verne was singing for Jesus and I was making personal appearances promoting both the movie and Him. Because we were both on the move and didn't happen to bump into each other again for some time, it was several months before I finally wrote that letter to Verne and Karen.

It simply said;

Dear Verne and Karen,
There is nothing to forgive.
I love you both.
In Him,
Randy

Any requests, comments, or inquiries for speaking engagements should be directed to:
Randy Bullock
Balsiger Literary Service
257 Brentwood Street
Costa Mesa, California 92627

About The Co-Author

Dave Balsiger, the co-author of this book, has ghost authored *The Satan Seller* (by Mike Warnke, Logos International - c. 1972), *One More Time* (by Don Musgraves, Bethany Fellowship - c. 1974), *The Back Side of Satan* (by Morris Cerullo, Creation House - c. 1973), and *Noah's Ark: I Touched It* (by Fernand Navarra, Logos International - c. 1974).

He has just completed a book tentatively entitled *Beyond Defeat* covering the life of James E. "Johnny" Johnson, black American who has served under California Gov. Ronald Reagan as Director of the Department of Veteran Affairs, and under former President Richard Nixon as the Vice-Chairman of the Civil Service Commission and as the Assistant Secretary of the Navy. Currently, he is co-authoring a seventh book entitled *On The Other Side* (by Marvin Ford).

His book, *The Satan Seller,* made number seven on the "National Religious Best Seller's List" during April, 1973 and sold 109,000 copies in 1973. His *Noah's Ark: I Touched It,* sold 35,000 copies during the first two months of sales.

He served as chief photographer and feature writer for the *Anaheim Bulletin* for two years. As a foreign feature correspondent for magazines and 13 southern California weekly newspapers, his assignments took him to over 45 countries on both sides of the Iron Curtain. For a year, he was the news editor of *Logos Journal* and has written features or photo stories for such publications as the *National Star, Time, Christian Bookseller, Orange County Illustrated, Money Doctor, Playland* and the *National Tattler.*

As a political science-journalism major, he attended Cypress Junior College (Cypress, CA), Pepperdine University (Los Angeles), Chapman World Campus Afloat (Orange, CA) and the International College in Copenhagen (Denmark).

He is listed in the 1972-73, 9th edition of *Who's Who in California* and the 1974-75, 38th edition of *Who's Who in America.*